EUCLID'S BOYS LEAGUE ALL-STARS

Bruce Double'u

ISBN:0-9831776-2-7
ISBN-13:978-0-9831776-2-3

The Ships Author, Bruce Double'u
Printed by CreateSpace, an Amazon.com company

CONTENTS

ACKNOWLEDGEMENTS

In memory of coaches:

Sam Manello (and Barb); Jim Penny; Ray
Markiewicz (who sent newspaper articles to the players);
Bob Mullin, Shirl Vernon, and Joe Zanghi

Thanks for their assistance:

John Sheridan and John Mocny;

Euclid Historical Museum, Shore Cultural Center, and

Euclid Public Library; the 1982 Little League rule book;

Paul Serra; and, also, to coaches and assistance from:

The Bells (Bill and Marlaine) and the Cubs scorebooks;

Howie Briggs Jr.; and more thanks and good fortune to and from:

Mom and dad (for always being there); the Grinsteads; brother Bret for
coaching the first championship t-ball team; and Euclid's baseball system.

This would never have been completed without all the continuous
memories, support and inspiration.

I would be remiss not to mention the book *The Echoing Green* by Joshua
Prager, thankful for the baseball history therein.

And, lastly, to Jeff and his mom – Mrs. Rose – who could not be there the
second time but who must have been watching...

To all the coaches and young players involved in organized youth
leagues, everywhere.

PROLOGUE

Six months before the U.S Hockey team completed their "Miracle on Ice" Winter Olympics Gold, a team of 12-year-old baseball players in a suburb of Cleveland, Ohio were competing to complete a three-tournament sweep – a "Triple Crown" of baseball victories that had never been accomplished in the Cuyahoga county community as well as the surrounding suburbs and counties involved.

The Euclid Boys League All-Stars had competed in one tournament per year for 17 years and that was in Garfield, Ohio also in Cuyahoga County. That tournament, alone, was difficult enough to win. In the early years Euclid would play their own American League versus National League All-Star game (just like the Major Leagues) and then would promote their best players for the Garfield Invitational Tournament that had begun play in 1957. Euclid would not host its own tournament until the summer of 1977; Willoughby Hills hosting their first tournament in 1974. So, by 2010 with three tournaments being played, it is still believed no other Euclid Boys League All-Star team won three tournaments in the same summer – and without losing a single game. And this does not – but should – include the same city of 10-year-olds – with, basically, the same players – who were two-for-two in tournament championships.

The following is based and inspired by a true story compiled from surviving newspaper articles stating the accomplishments of the Euclid Boys League All-Stars of the 1979 season and the success of those returning players as 10-year-old All-Stars. Some details of the games are survived solely by memory and their storybook endings "Only Hollywood would make-up." Some "descriptive" moments (Mayfield, for example, although an actual suburb in Ohio, does not have a community park as precisely depicted; but the description is intended to help describe the general look and feel of most suburban baseball fields in use in Northeast Ohio during the dog days of an August, 1977 summer) and some game-action have been "created" too, basically, introduce some of Euclid's players and coaches and to display the tempo of the games being played and how the young players collectively, personally, and sometimes emotionally, responded to the adversity of America's pastime.

In addition, glimpses of games recalled are, basically, combined relating, in general, the successes – or maybe a failure – a player may have had during the course of a four or five game tournament. While researching the teams the Euclid All-Stars played it was never discovered exactly who Euclid defeated in the third game of a tournament so, again, keep in mind "creative license" liberties were taken when "reenacting" segments of a game. The Final Game is directly recalled from the newspaper article – complete with the team photo – that appeared in the Euclid Sun Journal describing how Euclid scored their runs and included the brief recap of some of the other teams Euclid played in their "Triple Crown" tournament run. That game occurred, approximately, 95% as written to reach its accurately recorded final score. The Triple Crown article also mentioned: "The same team won eight in a row as 10-year-old All-Stars."

As for the players and the coaches all names have been changed with some players identified by "nicknames" used to describe that player's persona or style of play. Again, while most of the dialogue between the players and coaches may not be entirely true – although a portion, certainly, did occur or may have happened – the interaction between the characters is a fair representation of each individual player, coach or parent being portrayed allowing the reader a glimpse of the "reality" of these modest suburbanites and their proud, community achievement. The names of coaches, coach-fathers, spouses, and others – past and present – that assisted in the development of this book are preserved and referenced in the acknowledgments.

In the days and months preceding 1980 a "recession" had become part of the country's vernacular. Unlike anything the country had experienced since the Depression of the 1920's – until the recent banking bailouts, mortgage buyouts, and rise in unemployment – president Jimmy Carter announced the United States was facing a major "Crisis." At the time, the U.S.S.R was consistently emerging as the ominous, evil-red acronym and would unjustly invade Afghanistan for geo-political reasons ensuring the Communist power of its deviously manipulating reputation that, on this writing in 2011, resembles a, somewhat, eerie and strikingly familiar situation – without the Communism! Times may change but history, certainly, has a way of repeating itself. And let us not forget we were a mere three months away from the American Embassy in Iran being overrun by a rebel coup led by the Ayatollah Khomeini. The grey cloud hanging over the country loomed dark and would become, and feel, larger. Not much was going as planned or expected in the United States of America. A pride was missing in the country and in its localized communities.

But, in that summer of 1979 what Euclid's All-Stars accomplished has not been repeated. In a time when Atari video games were beginning to decline in effect and popularity, and Beta had not yet vanished from the home viewing public, fifteen 12-year-olds brought a community together – even if just a small percentage of that 70,000 census populace knew of them for the duration – by playing unflinchingly in one common goal: not to lose. For one summer (actually two) they united family and friends and each other in that collective belief. A local sports writer, at the time, put it simply and definitively in the Euclid Sun Journal: "Euclid's never-say-die 12-year-olds..." They always did seem to find a way to "comeback" even when the odds appeared to be against them.

With their city name guiding, encouraging and emblazoned in cursive and white across the chests of their red jerseys with white sleeves under sky blue hats (believe it or not), they succeeded together until there were no more games to play or win; and they never did beat themselves while pulling-off a minor miracle or two of their own.

THE 10-YEAR-OLDS

༺✻༻

August, 1977

Maple and fewer oak trees hung behind the baseball field surrounding the parking lot and the entrance way to the community park in Mayfield, Ohio. To the 10-year-olds participating in the tournament it seemed like the whole world should be watching when, if fact, there were no more than fifty parents and mostly younger children just old enough to be baseball fans and wish they could, someday, compete in the championship game of a baseball tournament.

Mayfield and their league of 10-year-old All-Stars were playing Euclid's 10-year-old All-Stars. To a player the focus was not only on the game but, also, somewhat of a subconscious effort to prolong their summer vacation as long as possible. They would begin school, again, the first week in September and to a 10-year-old playing baseball school was not a top priority. It was summer; it was fast pitch baseball; and they were the kind days better remembered to last longer, rather than thinking about the start of another school year.

Euclid had won their previous tournament – in Euclid – by winning four games in a row. All the tournaments in Cuyahoga and Lake County were single elimination (at that time) and Euclid was on a seven game winning streak heading into the final of their second tournament against the host team Mayfield. There had been some concern of a possible rainout and the game had been delayed to an 8 p.m. start. A hard rain covered the area early that morning and, as game time approached, only a light drizzle had fallen allowing the humidity of a summer evening in Ohio help dry the field; a sprinkling of local, drying agent – looking like cat litter – was barely visible on the field within the white lines of the batter's box and the dirt around second base.

With the continuing humidity and the dampness the evening had taken on a hazy-mugginess accentuated in no small part by the glare from the four light towers surrounding the baseball field. It would be the first time Euclid's 10-year-olds played under the glare of nighttime lights.

As the visitors approached the field the lights seemed to tower over the proceedings; everything enclosed by the close proximity of trees behind the three rows of bleacher-stands which were behind and to the left of the dugout-benches; a light tower directly behind the center of the backstop fence; and the backstop with its fence over hang to prevent delays and damage from too many foul balls landing in the parking lot. There was a steamy scent in the air from the blacktop parking lot leftover from the drizzle of warm rain. A short street of suburban homes could be seen well beyond the right field fence behind more distant trees. It smelled like summer; almost game time; the players nervous and anxious to start.

Euclid had played their previous three games on field #2 closer to the middle school that was situated at the other end of Mayfield's community park. They had to acclimate themselves quickly, and they instinctively noticed how relatively close the backstop was to home plate. It might not be an automatic advancement on a wild pitch to the "screen". The base runners would, certainly, have to be aware of this – even the fast ones!

The coaches watched the players and smiled as they saw them talking and pointing to the backstop. The players eyed some more as they entered the open-doorway to the fenced-in dugout. There was no cover. The fences were familiar, green and coarse, but not rusting. The four-foot high fence completely surrounded the baseball diamond and the outfield; out-of-play about six-feet from the left and right field foul lines. The 200 ft. signs on the dark green fences were situated just inside each foul pole. In center field the distance was the same.

On the bench Euclid's manager and third base coach opened what was left of his box of game balls. The bag of dirty, no *longer* game balls were practically used for infield and outfield practice. Another coach grabbed two scuffed balls from the torn, cloth bag zippered open. Both teams were given 10 minutes to warm-up. Mayfield's tournament championship game would, soon, be under way. The delays were finally over.

Euclid, to a player, did not need reminding how important it was for them to win. But, they were even more convinced and pleased to know they were involved in a "big" game when, upon arriving at Mayfield, they could see they were not playing on an "open" baseball field. They actually had a homerun fence to deal with which gave the competing players the impression of an important game being played at a well represented and organized facility – like the pros! The only time Euclid's 10-year-olds had played on a baseball field that was completely fenced-in was during their own tournament played on Euclid's Veteran's Field in Euclid, Ohio – and, then, the four games being played in that August, Mayfield Tournament. "Vet's Field" in Euclid was normally reserved for the 11 and 12-year-old division and the Fourth of July Tournament only. Euclid's 10-year-olds had yet to play on a grass infield and would not have that privilege – like most if not all of these young players – until high school.

After 8 p.m. the game was in progress and, except for the glare from the light poles beyond the outfield fence in left, center, right-field, and behind the backstop, the sun setting, only affected the player's vision, some, bringing a competitive if unfamiliar oddity to the game.

Heck, even Chicago's Wrigley Field did not play night games in 1977!

It was muggy, even for those not playing. The mosquitoes began their less than random agitation and the parents sprayed their cans of Bug-Off around the benches and on the skin that showed on their children's arms and over their thin, white sanitary socks below the knees. But not in the face! The players, gladly, turned their heads and closed their eyes as the wet spray fell on their uniforms, arms, and backs of their necks. They tried not to taste. The smell was strong enough.

Euclid scored first when the top of their order – seeing Mayfield's pitcher for the second time – in order: walked, singled (both advancing on a passed ball), single (another passed ball), and another single scored three runs. Euclid would eventually build a six-run lead. But, Mayfield came back. Euclid's number two pitcher had gotten wild, himself, in the fifth and the lead had been cut to two runs in the sixth. He had walked four and thrown two pitches to the screen, also. Mayfield only had two hits but they were both "get-me-over" strikes that accounted for three RBI. Mayfield might have scored more but a base runner tried to score from third on another wild pitch, but the fence was too close and the ball rolled back to the catcher getting the runner easily at the plate without a throw to the pitcher, who was covering. Euclid's catcher was able to tag the futile slide of the runner at home plate, himself.

Euclid was somewhat surprised by the wildness and the comeback, but they were not panicky. Although they had run-ruled two teams – a lead of 12 or more runs by the fifth-inning – the final in the Euclid Tournament had gone the scheduled seven innings. They had expected another close game in the Mayfield final, too.

"Let's get those runs back!"

"Noose pitching the last inning?" T.C. offered to be taken out of the game. "I'm tired."

"Noose" was the nickname for Jay Nusman, Euclid's #1 pitcher. By rule he had one-inning left in his 7-inning calendar week. He had allowed just one hit in six-innings of a 7-1 win in their previous game. Twelve of the eighteen outs were strike-outs! Kenney Richmond – normally the third-baseman, out-fielder and five-hitter – had pitched the last inning to finish the semi-final victory. Richmond threw hard but he showed some nervousness by walking the bases loaded before striking out the final batter with runners on second and third. He was jokingly teased for losing the shutout.

Richmond had laced a three-hopper to the fence in left-center earlier in the Mayfield final for a stand-up triple, walking home when a needless relay throw from the Mayfield shortstop sailed over the fence, banging against the bleacher-stands, well out-of-play.

"Looks like he throws hard..." Euclid's lead-off hitter noticed Mayfield's new pitcher warming-up.

"You guys can hit him," T.C, Euclid's #2 pitcher said. "You two have the highest averages on the team...that's why you're the first two hitters.

"Not anymore," Euclid's second-baseman said. "I don't have any hits today...just a walk."

"He throws as hard as Noose." Euclid's number two-hitter chewed on one of his cuticles.

"Yeah he does."

"C'mon, Kuiper, you can hit him." "Kuiper" was their lead-off hitter and second-baseman's nickname. He was consid-ered a good "glove man" for Euclid and Duane Kuiper was the reigning second-baseman for the local Cleveland Indians in Major League Baseball's American League.

Over a five-year-span from 1975-1979 Duane Kuiper had averaged 136 hits per season with the Indians en route to a career .271 batting average and a total of 917 base hits over an 11-year professional baseball career. But what he is, probably, best known for – besides good defense, although he never won a gold glove – is the 1 homerun he hit his entire career (off one-time Cy Young winner Steve Stone) while playing over 1000 thousand games and accumulating just under thirty-five hundred at-bats. He was, clearly, a fan favorite in his days with the Cleveland Indians, winning a Man of the Year Award and a Good Guy of the Year Award before departing to the National League and the San Francisco Giants by the 1982 season where he, eventually, became their game day broadcaster.

Mayfield was about a twenty minute drive on the highway to downtown Cleveland's Municipal Stadium where the Indians shared their polar-seasonal venue with the Football Browns. Although the Cleveland Indians never competed for a pennant in the 1970's they were still Major League players and respected. Every 10-year-old playing baseball in Northeast Ohio (pretty much) imagined playing professional baseball in Cleveland's, cavernous Municipal Stadium – day or night.

After striking out on three pitches, the 10-year-old "Kuiper" came back to the dugout shaking his head and trying to control tears of frustration from swelling in his eyes.

"I just couldn't see the ball good," he said, shaking his strawberry-blonde hair. "Damn!" He slammed his 27-ounce bat against the fence, rattling three other Louisville aluminum bats, the silver knobs and bats falling from their hole-perch in the backstop fence.

"Easy Tanner," it was yet another nickname for just about any 10-year-old on the team who used profanity or lost his temper somewhat out of character, unlike the "Bears" character from the 1976 movie who continually swore and displayed his temper in total character.

Players on the bench chuckled at the reference. Everybody pretty much thought Tanner in the movie was hysterical.

"He's not blonde enough to be Tanner," Cole Pembroke said somewhat out of character from his quiet perch on the bench, "or pissy enough," which sounded dangerously close to profanity to the 10-year-olds surrounded by adults, causing most of the players to look around to see if either coach or parent had heard the, somewhat, dirty slang comment. Apparently nobody heard and Pembroke was in the clear.

Pembroke and "Kuiper" had been teammates on the Steelers – an inappropriate name, for most, playing on a baseball team in Northeast Ohio. Pittsburgh's Pennsylvania Steelers of the NFL were ritually beating the home town Browns on every given Sunday in the 1970's leaving an extremely bad taste in the mouths of Cleveland's die-hard sports fans.

"Stay loose, Kuip..." Coach Billups said, reminding them they still had the lead and needed to concentrate and finish the game with confidence. "C'mon Christy," Mr. Billups clapped his hands and returned to the confines of the third-base coach's box. His nine-year-old son and wife were in the bleacher-stands, watching.

"He didn't throw a curveball, did he?" Christy had taken his fingertip from his mouth. It was somewhat of an unwritten rule that 10-year-olds were not supposed to throw curveballs to prevent hurting their young arms. But, still, good pitchers like "Noose" and T.C had thrown a couple of curveballs each during the course of the tournament games when they just *had* to get that four-hitter or the "big out". Actually, the one curveball T.C. had thrown in the sixth-inning bounced in the dirt near the plate and was responsible for a passed ball. The "curve", certainly, did not always work.

"No, I just swung at a fastball in the dirt." Euclid's second baseman was upset with himself. He had swung at a "ball" and only managed to foul-off a pitch. It was almost embarrassing. He never struck-out!

Christy turned on the first pitch he saw and the Mayfield third baseman fielded the one-hopper at his hip, turned his body towards first base without exposing his back and arched a head-high throw to first, getting Christy by a full step. Two-out!

T.C stepped to the plate intent on redeeming himself. He had not given-up three runs in one-inning in his brief but entire, two-year career in the Euclid Boys Baseball League, including the All-Star games. He was a bit down on himself, but did not show it. He would hit the ball hard somewhere. He just knew this. He forgot about the walks and the wild pitches he had thrown and thought about the task at hand; fixating on the release point his dad and coach taught him from the moment he saw his first overhand pitch. Elbow up. Hands still. The pitch came. Strike! He saw it. He was ready. T.C had long straight hair that – when dry – covered his ears. But, after pitching six-innings in mid-80 degree heat and humidity, his ears could be seen sticking out from between his stringy, wet hair. It made his hair appear darker than it was. His hair separated where it once covered his neck. He crouched in his stance as the pitch arrived and he swung: the ball was slightly more inside than he thought. Still, although the sting and the deadening clang heard from the ball hitting the bat too close to the handle was distinguishable and felt, the ball looped and tried to level upward to avoid Mayfield's second baseman. The infielder stabbed his back-handed glove across his body and snagged the ball as he stepped towards his defending base. He made the catch, remained on his feet, and scurried to his dugout, dropping the ball by the pitching rubber as he passed it.

Mayfield's pitcher looked marginally surprised by the rea-sonably hard contact two of Euclid's batters had made, but he shrugged and jogged alongside his infield teammates, stop-ping beyond the third base line in front of their fenced-in dug-out where all his Mayfield coaches and teammates huddled to cajole and inspire each other for a rally.

"It's only two runs...we can hit this guy! One, two, three, Mayfield...!" And twelve, thirteen hands dropped in unison from the circle of their huddle, scattering and clapping. The first batter of the bottom-half of the 7th pinned-on his helmet and prepared him self to hit from within the remains of the white on-deck circle, swinging an aluminum bat with an additional 4-ounce "doughnut" snug around the barrel.

"Noose" stood on the rubber ready to throw. Euclid's #1 pitcher was a big lefty, especially by 10-year-old standards. He reared back and his arm whipped towards the plate. Pop! Mayfield's hitters could not help but, noticeably, move on their bench seats. There was a murmur. Noose threw again. Pop! His catcher's glove felt the sting.

Noose had also hit the game's only homerun in the fourth inning, pulling a pitch over the right-center field fence. There had been some hesitation by the two umpires because the ball was not hit that high. They converged, quickly, wondering if the ball had bounced over the fence, but everyone concurred – including the stunned Mayfield team. The ball had cleared the fence and landed well over two-hundred feet away! That had made the score 5-0 and appeared to be the back breaker. Richmond, then, had followed with his laser-triple, scoring on the throwing error.

At shortstop, Tommy Lotts could not help but smile under the brim of his sweaty hat, his long, brown hair doing the same. "He's not even throwing hard yet," he said to T.C, playing third in the likelihood no one would pull the ball to him, forcing his tired arm to make a throw. But he had too good a glove not to be put in the infield and, certainly, would not be left on the bench. They could not afford to rest T.C that much. Besides, this was the last game and there was no tomorrow until next summer.

The coaches made their last, everybody is supposed to

play, substitutions. This was not much of an issue with All-Star teams, but the best players almost never got substituted. With T.C moving to third base Kenney Richmond relocated to centerfield.

Noose turned his back to home plate and rubbed the feel of the baseball into his left hand. He looked at his second baseman, his head down, kicking dirt.

"Hey, forget the strikeout," Noose said. "We got the lead." Noose replaced his baseball glove onto his right hand and pounded the baseball into its pocket. "Kuiper" acknowledged him and pounded his fist into his glove.

Tommy Lotts hollered from his shortstop position: "One, two, three, Noose."

"Bottom of the order: eight, nine, one!" Coach Billups reminded from the bench.

Noose struck-out the first hitter on three pitches and Euclid's Eight erupted on the field.

Noose followed with two quick strikes on the nine-hitter, when the Mayfield batter surprised everyone by squaring to bunt despite knowing, by rule, he would be called out if he just foul-tipped the oncoming fastball he had seen twice and barely reacted to.

T.C had been playing a step in front of the bag and had not moved back but a step even after the second strike. It was the nine-hitter, after all. He watched the ball float toward him and in his mind he knew if the ball went foul the batter would be out.

Noose took a step toward the ball in following through with

his pitching motion, but knew he could not field the bunted ball. The trajectory of the ball hugged the line, airborne, in fair territory.

"Let it go foul...!" Was the call of instruction from the coaching bench...but T.C had the view. He had the angle. The ball was straight, and floating, and started on its downward trajectory. T.C exploded to the ball, not an ounce of fatigue visible from his pitching legs. Within five steps T.C was at a sprint as he reached down, glove inside the foul line, and picked-up the ball in his webbing, clean and clear before the ball could make its mark in the dirt.

"Batter's out!"

The first base side of the field escalated the celebration as Euclid's bench of five players and three coaches cheered along with a synchronized yell from the bleacher-stands; parents clapping three-rows deep.

Noose smiled. He could get nowhere near the bunt attempt and he said so to T.C. "Nice play."

"Top of the order," Mr. Billups reminded, again.

Noose blew two fastballs by Mayfield's lead-off batter. Again, the hitter barely budged as the pitches went passed. Noose wound and arm-whipped another strike and the hitter stepped and swung his right-handed bat and the ball bounced twice and rolled to Tommy Lotts at shortstop. He stepped to the ball, fielding it before the short hop, and stepped and threw side-armed to first-baseman Harrison "Harry" Dodd. At 5 foot 2 he was an inch or two shorter than their starting first baseman Dan "Baby Face" Grossman, who had played the first four innings. Harry's own, dark freckles seemed to brighten as his eyes became bigger, watching as the side-arm-throw arrived low. But, if his stretch might not have been quite as long as Grossman's, Harry had little problem with a minor scoop of the baseball. With his right foot on the bag Harry bent, easily, and stepped forward with baseball and a puff of dirt in his glove. He continued to toe the bag as the hustling Mayfield runner was slow by a full step.

The field umpire called the out and Harrison – with arms and glove and ball in the air – ran toward his dugout and "Noose," who was already near Euclid's dugout by the first base line. That was as far as they got for the moment was absorbing. The players on the bench came out of the dugout and circled their pitcher, slapping him on the back. Coach Billups and Coach Charles – the father of T.C – slowly walked out of the dugout, smiling. They shook hands with each other.

Coach "Z" smiled and surveyed the stands and the field. He felt better because his "Steelers" had not lived up to the name of the NFL namesake of multiple Super Bowl wins. The baseball Steelers had been stopped short of the finals despite a great start and high expectations. Somehow their pitching had fallen short.

Eventually, the eight remaining 10-year-old Euclid All-Stars on the field gathered by their pitcher near the first base line in a circle of jubilant bodies, listening to the applause and smiles from their parent's in the stands.

"Okay, boys, go shake hands," Coach "Z" said, pointing

towards the Mayfield bench. Coaches Billups and Charles nodded with continued smiles of approbation. "That was a great game."

After the line of smiling faces slapped hands with the glum faces of their foes, each player arriving or approaching home plate, repeating, "Good game, good game, good game," the celebration proceeded with some jumping and a few shouts of joy.

And the parents looked at each other, each a little surprised how proud and how good they actually felt. Their sons had done it! Euclid had done it! They had won two tournaments without losing a game! Mr. Nusman could be seen repeating the record to Mr. Richmond who nodded, their wives close by – They had gone 8-0!

LITTLE LEAGUE RULES

❦

It 1979 Euclid's Boy's League was not affiliated, officially, with Little League. It had been, briefly, but by the 1950's Euclid and the surrounding Cuyahoga and Lake Counties were simply local "Boys" Leagues which, in varying degrees, became a mild topic of contention. It was, in a sense, its own baseball entity, but adhered to Little League Baseball and its rules that had grown in immense popularity since its modest upbringing in Williamsport, Pennsylvania in 1939. Little League had been, initially, a localized league that grew, exponentially, from the Midwest on out. It quickly moved eastward. And spread to the west.

A Boys Baseball League, by name, caused controversy, not so much from borrowing and implementing the Little League rules, but because, in its name, it may have seemed to represent its own baseball league, or worse, a gendered "club." Some suggested, maybe rightfully so, that by name a Boys League was unfair and not politically correct by way of being sexist. The issue was very quickly resolved when the time came: when a girl and her parents asked if their daughter could play in Euclid Boys League she was permitted without hesitation. In 1979 *Laura* – playing for the Euclid Boys League *White Sox* – positioned herself admirably at catcher and first base and participated in the Euclid 4th of July Tournament as a representative of Euclid's All-Star B Team.

There was some talk of changing the name, again, but that time never came. Girls continued to join and play, when they desired.

As a matter of point and intent a Boys League would certainly aspire to thrive – not necessarily with as much publicity – but with the respect and All-American recognition that has been bestowed upon Little League: In 1964 the House of Representatives and the Senate so approved of the expansion of Little League that they signed a law that granted Little League Baseball a Congressional Charter of Federal Incorporation. High praise indeed for any sports organization let alone a youth league. The law was signed to protect the name and insignia of Little League by the President of the United States, himself: Lyndon Baines Johnson.

So, it is no wonder the Boys Leagues of Northeast Ohio wished to proceed with the hopes of structuring their leagues with the integrity that Little League had accomplished itself.

Euclid's Boys League began organized play in 1949. And only minor rule changes would be made by the rotating Commissioners and Officers of the Northeast Ohio youth league as the years progressed and the league grew from twelve to sixteen teams, et cetera.

Fences, when constructed, would not necessarily be 200 ft. from left to center to right-field (Little League, eventually, distanced their dimensions to 225 ft. – the kids were hitting too many homeruns!) while some suburban cities would have fences 200 feet from home plate (there is more than some speculation some fences were closer) evenly distributed around their outfields. These "baseball fields" would also be used for the 9 and 10-year-old division.

Euclid's Veterans Field had dimensions with "alleys" in left-center and right-center with centerfield being the deepest part of the playing field, like in a Major League Baseball park (not as large, of course). The outfield dimensions at "Vet's Field" in Euclid were 210 in left and 220 in right field while a sign in straight-away center read 260 ft. There were no signs in left-center or right-center but a safe estimate would be 245 to 250 ft. "to the alleys."

Veteran's Field was located behind "The Manor" (becoming Tizzano's) at the intersection of East 260th Street and Tungsten Avenue in Euclid Ohio, about two-hundred yards from Euclid Avenue (Route 20). A concession stand had been built alongside the immediate location of the league's new, proud ball park. Together, they re-opened by 1966. The previous concession stand – which had been located behind Roosevelt Elementary school and off Arbor Ave. – had been situated in a small garage right at the edge of one of Euclid's local, growing neighborhoods beside the "old" Veteran's Field. As more homes were built Veteran's Field was moved to the other side of town, off East 260th Street, where the concession stand ditched the garage-look and was replaced by a more modern, tool shed, red barn appearance. It was constructed complete with a large rectangular window that would be propped open by two large wood extensions with a small but level foldout counter where straw and napkin containers set. It was open all game days. "Hotdog Day" came once a season and acknowledged and honored the players by giving them one hotdog, a small bag of chips, and a soda, free, on that day after they played. There was an elevated, wooden deck built behind the backstop that grew into a covered scorer's table with an electronic box, inside, to control the score board just beyond the 260 ft. sign in center field. It was no coincidence the center-field distance was the same as the "Eastside" street number Vet's Field could see in the distance, just beyond The Manor.

It was the field any and all Euclid Boy's League participant wanted to play on; and one of four fields that was conveniently located by a school that a majority of players did or would attend. There were two other "open-field" baseball diamonds behind Forest Park Junior High (and Middle School, as time passed) where a rolling homerun would bound into that school's 440 yd. track. Inside the oval track was the Forest Park "Rangers" football field complete with the old, H-shaped goal posts, occasionally, a game day extra point might be converted by a 7th, 8th, or 9th-grader. In late August when the regular, Boys League baseball season was winding down, a few early bird students could be seen training for the upcoming junior high school track season.

Tungsten Avenue, still, twists east behind (what was) both fields and turns into a residential row of apartment-condominiums where the street turns, again – after a mile or so – as a conduit to Euclid Ave. and East 260th St.

The other field, on the other side of Tungsten Avenue, facing the playground and Thomas Jefferson Elementary School beyond left and left-center-field, was affectionately called "T.J." T.J did not have a homerun fence until a makeshift brown, wood-and-wired fence was built specifically for the Euclid 4th of July tournaments of the mid-to-late 1980's. The outfield dimensions attempted to resemble Vet's Field, yet the wood fence was shorter in height. Part of the reason the fence was built was to prevent the ball from rolling into Euclid's mini-Police Station's back yard. Located beyond right and right-center the play might be called "dead" by rule. Then the umpires would have to converge and risk the ruling of sending a runner back to his (or her) previous base when in all practicality the ball in the station-yard would have amounted to a homerun for the batter, causing too much game day controversy. At least with the brown, wooden fence in use, the only way a ball could reach the station's back yard was by a batted ball clearing the fence; or if the ball bounced over the fence it would cause less commotion, by a more common ground rule: the ground rule double with all runners advancing two bases.

Some time around the new millennium there were reservations over the land and the necessity for Veteran's Field to continue to co-exist with the veterans' annual participation on Euclid Boys League's opening day ceremonies. The Vet's and their sponsorship folded at the mere suggestion of their significance and the importance of their notoriety – and Veteran's Field was razed for the possibility of additional parking spaces and what is now a field of green grass and an uneven row of trees beside the Lanly Company Warehouse that had set horizontal – and well out of play – to Vet's Field's left field line. Somewhat coincidentally, or ironically (oddly?), even the Palisades Bowling Alley which had been located on the other side of the shared parking lot, and had been there as long as Veteran's Field, if not longer, also closed down. The old Palisades building remains, has been maintained, and became a place of worship.

But, as far as other mainstream rules as developed by Little League, The Euclid Boys League decided to integrate 7-inning games as opposed to Little League's 6-inning games with the 12-run-rule in place for the 5th inning instead of the 4th inning 10-run-rule.

Little League Rules suggested 25 ft. of foul territory behind the first and third base lines to their respective fences, and 25 ft. from home plate to the backstop. This recommendation was rarely close to that distance in Leagues in Northeast Ohio. The farthest backstop to home plate may have registered 20 feet and concaved toward each opening to a dugout-bench. None of the fields ever – in Boy's League – structured an actual dugout where the teams walked down steps to get to their benches. All the "dugout" benches were at ground level but, occasionally, there would be a baseball complex or a community park of baseball fields that covered their benches with a cement roof and back wall. And, if a field was fenced-in, the first and third base foul lines were no farther than 10 feet to their out-of-play fences. The fields were definitely much more compact than in Little League with just enough bleacher-stand space (usually made of a hard aluminum that could still burn with a summer sun and, at least, did not splinter themselves or anyone sitting on them) for the parents to collectively sit. Some would bring lawn chairs and sit and look through the four-foot-high fences, when applicable; or when the fences were not a part of the field boundaries would position themselves safely outside the "out-of-play" boundaries. Some parents and fans would just stand for as long as they could stand it.

But, the Little League rules that mattered most were the field dimensions as written in distance for the base paths and the pitching distance to home plate. Base-to-base the agreed upon distance was 60 ft. There would be no stealing a base until a pitcher's pitch reached the batter. There were no lead-offs. And the length from the pitcher's "rubber" to the rear point of home plate figured to be 46 ft.; the rubber pitching-plate a rectangular slab of what should be whitened rubber, 18 in. by 4 in. in diameter; the "mound" 6 in. above home plate; home plate 17 in. wide facing the pitcher and the 12-inch square of home plate coming to a point at 8-inch intervals; the first and third base lines intersecting at the 12-inch home plate intervals.

And the baseball equipment, protection a priority: bats, catcher's gear, the baseballs, themselves, legal for use.

No bat would be permitted longer than thirty-three inches in length or more than 2¼ inches in diameter. Each baseball no less than 5 ounces and no more than 5¼ ounces in weight, and no less than 9 inches nor more that 9¼ inches in circumference. The catcher, of course, would need the proper mask, helmet, chest protector and shin guards to protect them from foul tips and other possible baseball collisions.

It was during the 1976 Major League season Steve Yeager – in the midst of playing one of 14 successful campaigns with the highly competitive Los Angeles Dodgers appearing in four World Series and developing the reputation as a defensive specialist who, also, "managed" his pitchers as well as being considered the best throwing catcher in the game by many of his peers – was struck in the esophagus by teammate Bill Russell's shattered bat while waiting in the on-deck circle. After needing surgery to remove the splintered wood Yeager and the Dodger's trainer, Bill Buhler, invented and patented the "throat protector" that hung from the catcher's mask. By 1979 Euclid Boy's League had implemented the Steve Yeager throat protector as a mandatory piece of protective equipment. It would not be long for catcher's masks to be seen with actual extensions built onto the frame of the catcher's mask – and the eventual ingenuity to incorporate the modern day, hockey mask – instead of the additional dangling-plastic in front of the Adam's apple. And Euclid Boys League, like Little League, would take whatever precautions necessary to ensure the safety of their young players whenever the situation arose along with the technological advancements.

In 1986 Steve Yeager retired from baseball and, soon, was a Minor League coach affiliated with the Los Angeles Dodgers. By 2007 he was managing the independent league, A-level Long Beach Armada and was said to be instrumental in the development of Dodger All-Star Russell Martin's (bought and playing for the New York Yankees by the 2011 season) conversion from 3rd baseman to catcher .

Today, Steve Yeager can be seen on cable or DVD portraying Coach Temple "waving home" Willie Mays Hayes in the 1989 Major League movie finale, where he also was on-hand as a baseball advisor, naturally. It also may be interesting to note Steve Yeager *is* related to "uncle" Chuck Yeager the Test-Pilot who dramatically broke the Sound Barrier in 1947 – a fine family accomplishment to add to the collection, indeed.

But, arguably, the most efficient and influential rule adopted from Little League was the innings pitched limit. Expanded to the highest levels it can be easily argued that Little League inspired the Major League organizations to adopt this pitch-count mentality in the greatest effort to help preserve and elongate the careers of their "prize" signings and "bonus-babies." Never again will a Major League pitcher pitch 300-innings in one season for fear of him wearing out before his contract expires. The blown-out shoulder or elbow does not just shorten the pitcher's career anymore but the bankbooks of the owners who still must pay the guaranteed money of the countless multi-year contracts!

Euclid Boys League decided 7-inning games would be played instead of 6-innings, as is written in Little League, by the 1968 season. So, the only difference in a Boys League pitcher's calendar week was he or she could pitch 7-innings, Sunday through Saturday, instead of six. Everything else remained the same: If a pitcher pitched four innings plus that player must rest three full days, Sunday and pitch again on Thursday. A pitcher could pitch three innings or less and only need one day of calendar rest, Sunday and pitch Tuesday. The delivery of a single pitch would constitute an inning.

The reasoning behind the rules reads two-fold: safety and domination. Again, the top priority is the safety of all players and their young arms. But, also, it might seem fair to give other players a chance while preventing one team from using the same overpowering advanced-mature pitcher to win game-after-game ... kind of like today's pitcher's in women's, underhand, fast pitch softball who seem to pitch, literally, every game. Is the strain on these talented, "pioneering" female pitchers – Cy Young and Walter Johnson pitched 400 innings in a season during baseball's "infancy" – that much less than a grown male throwing the magic number 100 pitches, overhand, every five days at the professional level? Again, it seems to be about ownership and economics, although medical personnel have stated their belief the under-handed style of fast-ball, body torqueing, change-up pitching is nowhere near as physically demanding as the overhand follow through of muscle stretches and ligament strains. Time – and the changing "growth" of all sports – will tell.

In all sports safety is a major and, you would think, cost-worthy issue. In baseball and the Little Leagues around the world – as it has grown even more so than just the eastward and westward expansion in the United States, but North America, in general; and Japan, Puerto Rico, and the Dominican Republic; and the many Central and South American countries where "soccer" and baseball have become the #1 and #2 sports, respectively; where the development of Venezuelan baseball players is approaching remarkable (Concepcion, Aparicio, Guillen and Vizquel; and Bobby Abreu and Victor Martinez to name just a few from past and present) – and the competitive teams from smaller nations like Chinese Tapei (Taiwan); or the entire island community of Curacao where its youth has competed for Little League World Series Championships despite a population no larger than Euclid and its namesake, southern neighbor, within northeast Ohio.

But, with all this success from smaller venues of organized baseball there have been far too many warning signs that, still, has not prevented the inevitable fatality from occurring (a 13-year-old was killed in 2007 in the U.S when a line drive off an aluminum bat struck the youth in the chest). Any parent or student of the game cannot help but wonder when or if a change should be made to constitute what is a legal or safe baseball bat and at what level of competition. It appears that multiple fatalities must occur before a resolution is finally reached where a pitcher does not need to fear being hit by a batted ball from an aluminum bat that simply has too good a "hot" or "sweet spot" within its barrel; or the constant fracturing and, now, exploding and spiraling barrels of wooden bats impaling an opponent, pitcher, or base runner.

Steve Yeager was somewhat fortunate "only" his esophagus was damaged. And that was back in 1976! Major League baseball may have been fortunate no other baseball players died from a baseball "beaning" after 1920 when the Cleveland Indians Ray Chapman was hit in the temple by a rising, submarine-styled-pitch from New York Yankees pitcher Carl Mays. It is hard to believe baseball could not construct or invent a batting helmet sooner than 1956 when the batting helmet finally became mandatory – but not in both leagues! And that was 36 years after Chapman's baseball-related death.

It has been over 30 years now since Steve Yeager took his teammates shattered bat in the throat. In 2010 Shawn Colvin of the Chicago Cubs was almost impaled running down the third-base line, innocently, he thought, attempting to score a run, when a teammates bat burst, split, and like a spinning, wooden joust put a hole in his chest deep enough to allow too much outside air to enter. He had to be taken to the hospital and closed, quickly. It ended the three weeks that remained in Shawn Colvin's baseball season. Again, it sounds like he was fortunate it was not much worse. College pitchers and high school pitchers have been maimed and rendered comatose by line drives hit back at them without a movement of self-preservation to avoid the ball. They, simply, could not avoid or never did see a ball that ricochets in the returning direction faster and harder than any pitcher can wind and throw the ball themselves. And, many of today's successful pitchers can reach 90 miles-per-hour on their speed gun fastballs. Still, more, seem to be teasing loo M.P.H which used to be rare except for the few Nolan Ryan's of the world.

The not-so-secret to the aluminum bat's success is in its hollow core. That, and thinner handles allowing for improved bat speed and an even distribution of weight coupling with a bat that, rarely, cracks or breaks and the baseball has no other alternative but to eject from the lighter-metal-aluminum bats in a much less constricting or compressed manner than wood bats. And with wood bats – in the attempt to counteract the lack of a "give" or the "trampoline effect" – which seem to be breaking at a ridiculous rate, the safety issues of wood bats, appear, clear and easy to fix. The handles of the bats are shaved too thin – by the players – to promote and initiate more bat speed, and the wood most commonly used is maple. The players love the "live", "sweet spots" on the maple bats but indications reveal the maple bats tend to break at a much more, highly visible rate. Ash seems to be safer, splitting but not exploding like maple's deficiency. Here is a safe bet that Little League will not allow its Little Leaguers to ever use an aluminum bat longer than 33 inches and will, likewise, never approve of using a more "lively" titanium-style bat (titanium was banned in all leagues from softball to hardball in the mid 1990's) for the benefit of the hitter. Technology, certainly, will draw the safety line somewhere before we see a 12-year-old shaving the handle of his new, wooden bat before he ever takes a razor to his face.

It, also, may be noteworthy to mention a substance called polymer can be – and is – used to help "soften" the hollow core of aluminum bats helping to alleviate a few miles-per-hour from the more "lively" aluminum bats while not deterring the metal from its protective alloys that maintain an aluminum bats strength and durability without improving its performance. Simply put the aluminum bats can be made cost efficiently, and more durable than wood bats, and can be produced with the safety measures in mind without making them less-productive than wood bats (It should be noted the NCAA did regulate safer, aluminum bats for the 2011 season).

And, of course, there is no avoiding the travesty of steroids running rampant at far too many levels of sports, causing more safety and cheating issues. Gambling and "throwing" games cannot be tolerated although players *seem* to be paid well enough to avoid these temptations where only rumors occasionally spread on behalf of professional athletes (like the local rumor of a college quarterback "fixing and losing" the National Championship game to receive a paid-in-full, condominium in Texas, because he knew he would not be drafted until after the 3rd round in the upcoming NFL draft, therefore, not being offered the designated "signing bonus" top draft picks receive). But, these are, somewhat, separate issues; and, like noted, sometimes just rumors.

The growing risk of plunging a syringe into someone's blood stream to enhance sounded wrong when football players' decades ago (see Lyle Alzado) were growing into psychotically, pumped-for-the game machines wound-up to initiate the game day havoc; the preparation to unleash them from their symbolic cages with the savage, war paint stereotype that, apparently, is accurate. It seems a bit odd baseball allowed their "professionals" to play well into a "Steroid Era" that had been admitted. But, everyone has the right to work especially when there are large sums of money circulating (as of this writing Manny Ramirez had been suspended – for the second time – for testing positive, prompting his immediate retirement).

It is probably safe to say, at this point, that Jose Canseco's book *Juiced* should not be seen as just a farfetched, personal vendetta, money-maker, by an ego-maniac who was looking for recognition and benefits after his own playing day facts were well behind him. The truth about the players and the "usage" are, certainly, coming to the forefront.

Pete Rose, Major Leagued baseball's all-time hits leader and not permitted in Cooperstown's Hall of Fame for lying about gambling and *not* cheating or fixing games, received a far worse punishment. He loved baseball as much as he love(s) (loved) himself. At least he was not a slave to its drug-addled, hypocritical successes. He was –and still is – a proud yet suffering slave to the game.

Today, most if not all professional baseball players take no shame in watching the Little League World Series in their clubhouses before they play another of their 162, supposedly, more important games. They know and remember the feeling of being a part of that early All-American, and now, International competition. It represents the player's roots; their upbringing; and, basically, why they play baseball. From the very start they simply loved it just for the game itself and not for what may have transpired sense. They are successful because of it. They can root for their state, region, or the city they are from and easily remember just how enjoyable the game has been to be a part of; the game becoming a part of them; of being a part of an aging standard that reminds grown men of their youth and the "kid that remains" stirring within; their wood bats and leather gloves part of a performance that has become an extension of their very being from its primitive, honest and adolescent form to the purity of all that remains from those early, untainted summer days; and the recognition to be grateful for; and the dream of greatness while learning to participate in the games fluid tempo with "controlled aggression"; striving to, one day, participate on a brisk-chilly night in October's greatest team achievement, "The Fall Classic."

And as Joe Jackson – his star to the Hall of Fame shattered by an era of gamblers, crooked ball players and stingy, monopolizing owners, lowlighted by the "Black Sox throwing" the 1919 World Series to the Cincinnati Reds – said in the movie Eight Men Out (based on the book by Eliot Asinof, the close of the 1920 season when the players were, officially, expelled from baseball, excluding them from one final chase for the American League pennant) "I'd play for food, if they'd just let me."

After all, the Little Leagues and the Euclid Boys Leagues of the world really do "rule." The love of something always begins somewhere.

GETTING THE CALL

⚜

Late June, 1979

Mr. Mason was already planning ahead. He knew, because of the calendar week, they were going to need a third pitcher to "eat" some innings in Euclid's Firecracker Invitational the week surrounding the Fourth of July.

"With the kids playing league games, still, we're going to have to find someone to start a game." Mr. Mason looked at his assistant coaches, Mr. Manta and Mr. Sherwin, for advice.

"We still got to get the roster to fifteen," Coach Sherwin said. "How many players got votes from the other nine managers?"

"Well, let's see," Mr. Mason began, "there were a total of 160 votes from 16 managers who selected twenty-one different players."

"And how close are we now?"

"We are down to twenty!" Mr. Mason said.

"I noticed the improvement in the new kid in the league, Michael Blake. They just moved here and it might be a nice gesture too, since they're new to Euclid."

"Nice gestures are – nice – but is he good? I don't remember playing against him," the assigned, tournament Manager said to Coach Manta.

"He probably didn't pitch against you when you played them. He's a tall kid – a lefty – and he, really, just learned how to pitch. He cares and, if he can get passed the nerves, he could be effective. Believe me if you'd faced him you'd remember. Newton's son – coaching the Yankees now – faced Blake recently and he shut-them-out."

"He doesn't hit very well, though, does he?" Coach Mason added, somewhat dismissively.

"What?" Coach Manta questioned, somewhat surprised. "He's on quite a few ballots."

"This is good to know...we still have a game left against the Orioles. I expect he'll pitch this time," the manager of the first place A's said.

"What about the days he doesn't pitch?"

"We can worry about that when the time comes. The way it looks we can put him at first-base when Nusman pitches. It shouldn't be difficult to find time for all the kids to play." This was, also, a minimum requirement rule for a player participating in a Euclid Boys League game: every player must play in the field for three outs or be permitted one at-bat per game. Although in tournament games the rules – as far as playing time – were not strictly enforced.

"What about Pembroke, or Dakalos, or Grossman? They can pitch."

"Dakalos seems to have lost his enthusiasm...he keeps talking about a sore arm, probably, from throwing too much side-arm junk."

"Pembroke and Grossman we could always use in an emergency."

"Mr. Billups has the Cubs playing well and Pembroke is his best pitcher."

"He throws hard, but he can't throw a curve, yet."

"Well, we'll see."

"And we have Kenney Richmond, too. We could always use him at some point," Mr. Mason reminded them. "Okay, well, if we put Michael Blake on the roster we still have four openings. The players from the 10-year-old team are in. The managers, basically, voted the obvious ones in, already, so that's good. And I still think Stephen Marsch deserves a chance."

"Four players from the Athletics...?" Coach Sherwin questioned.

"We're still undefeated," Coach Mason reminded, smiling, "and he's a good reason why."

"Shouldn't we have a rep from every team?" Coach Manta asked.

"That's not in the rules...and this ain't the Major Leagues. I don't know why they do that," Coach Sherwin said, questioning The Show, "The best players don't necessarily play in the All-Star game. Letting the fans vote is bad enough."

"And who's gonna' catch?"

"Dakalos can catch."

"Yes, but he doesn't like too...hurts his knees."

"Is he gonna' be okay to play?"

Two of the coaches laughed.

"He'll be fine. The best all-around player on the Braves," Mr. Manta said, reminding them why they were there.

"Grossman can catch, too."

"You saw him catch?"

"Yes, in a game."

"He is valuable," Coach Mason admired, "but we should still have someone who caught all the time during the regular season... someone who's not new to it."

"I see Shuman on a couple ballots. He's a catcher? He pitches too?"

"He's not gonna' pitch," the prediction came bluntly.

Mr. Manta remembered the two catchers that were on the 10-year-old team that were not in the league anymore. They both had moved. Mr. Manta's son was eleven and he wondered if he would be good enough to make the team the following year. Maybe he should try converting him to catcher. Catchers were beginning to seem harder to come by. Mr. Manta concluded it was good the manager and coaches were aware the current All-Star team needed a catcher on the squad with plenty of game day experience. He thought he had one from the Phillies.

"Oh, yeah, skinny kid...he's been catching for a couple years. He moves good behind the plate, but I wonder about his hitting, too. That's probably why he's not on more ballots," Coach Sherwin said, looking for Coach Manta to respond.

"Okay to Shuman?" Coach Mason asked.

"Bob Shuman," Mr. Manta answered on behalf of his catcher.

"Stephen Marsch...?" The Manager asked, again, for approval from his assistants.

The assistant coaches hesitated.

"And Michael Blake...?"

Mr. Sherwin looked at Mr. Manta.

"Maybe we should have a tryout-practice," Mr. Manta suggested. "It might help weed-out these last three or four players."

"We're gonna' have to cut somebody, then, assuming everyone shows-up," Mr. Mason said.

"If a borderline player doesn't make it, then..." Mr. Sherwin did not need to finish his thought.

"You know what? We need a player that hasn't played the infield all year that's not going to complain about playing sparingly and in the outfield."

"It sounds like we're going to have an alternate list too."

"We have some phone calls to make, gentlemen."

"Do you want to split those calls in half, three ways?" Coach Sherwin offered.

Manager and Coach stopped to look, smiling at the helpful yet mathematical impossibility.

"You know what I mean."

"Who do you think you are, Yogi Berra?"

"That settles it...we'll call twenty-one players for the tryout and take it from there..."

"Who else is gonna' be there?"

"We're meeting at Vet's Field," Mr. Mason said. Of the seven players he called six had been on the 10-year-old All-Star team and four were from his Athletics. "You'll meet your teammates – most I'm sure you know already. Mr. Sherwin and Mr. Manta will be there, too."

"Okay."

"I'm assuming you're accepting the invitation for the try-out?" Mr. Mason was smiling from his end of the phone. He waited for the lone representative from the Red Legs to respond, milking the reply.

"Yes, I was there 2 years ago. I'll be there."

"Are you sure?" He could not help but instigate. He was well aware of the second baseman's enthusiasm.

"Hell yeah...can't wait."

"Okay, then, see you Saturday at two. And don't swear."

"Oh, sorry, Saturday at two...got it."

"Michael, we want you to come to a tryout for the Euclid All-Star team," Coach Manta said. "We might need you to pitch."

"Really...? My parents were talking about going to Florida later in the summer. Would that make a difference?"

"Not for the 4th of July tournament."

"Okay. I'll be there..."

"Is this Casey Urzak?"

"Yes. Who's this?"

"This is Mr. Sherwin from Euclid Boy's League."

"Oh, you're one of the coaches from the..."

"That's right...the Red Sox. Would you be interested in trying out for the All-Star team? We have a practice Saturday at two?"

"Yes. Yes, I would."

"I think it's fair to say we may have you as an alternate depending on what happens with some of the other players."

"That's okay. I'll be there for the tryout. Thanks."

"See you at Vet's Field." Mr. Sherwin began to expect, more and more, all the kids would show-up.

The players began to arrive, almost all receiving rides from their parents. Two of the players rode their bicycles, living no more than a mile or two from the field: Sam Brocco, a wiry, dusty blonde, whom some considered somewhat of a "hotdog", and Dan Grossman whose round baby face had stretched along with the three inches grown since he was ten. He was in a mild stage of acne and his voice had deepened. It caused an early, embarrassing moment with Coach Manta who had helped coach the team during the 4th of July (Firecracker) Tournament two years earlier.

"Hello," Mr. Manta had said as he reached out a hand to greet Grossman who would be 13 after August 1st, allowing him to participate as a 12-year-old. "Baby Face" Grossman would be no more as he was one of three players on the roster that was actually preparing to enter the 8th grade, not the 7th grade. The other two were Tommy Lotts and Tim Lake. "I'm coach Manta, you are...?"

"Coach..?" Grossman paused, wondering for a second if his former All-Star coach was kidding with him. When there was a chuckle amongst the players, all knowing who Grossman was, there was a correlated reminder of "It's Danny" and Coach Manta shook his head in disbelief, continuing to shake the young player's hand as Dan Grossman, baby face or not, continued to smile like he always did.

"You changed...I'm sorry...it's good to see you...I think I recognized you last month when we played...my goodness. We didn't get to talk though."

"You beat us pretty bad that day," Grossman said, smiling.

"Well, there'll be no more of that. Isn't that something?" Coach Manta continued in his amazement and directed it towards Coach Sherwin, who revealed a smirk, well aware how the inevitable change in some of the players was instrumental and part of all their development.

"They're getting bigger, that's for sure."

Once the players were seated in the stands and role-call completed, Mr. Mason allowed Mr. Manta to speak to the players and arrange the upcoming practice-tryout. Mr. Sherwin sat and, listened too, behind his thick black mustache that turned around his mouth, pointing downward.

"We're gonna' jog across the street to T.J since it's after two and take some batting practice and some infield. Sound good?"

Everybody nodded in agreement, picked-up their gloves and rubber or plastic-cleat shoes, and jogged outside the fence along the left field line and across Tungsten Avenue to T.J. The coaches left their cars in the lot in front of the Palisades

Bowling Alley. Grossman and Brocco pushed their bicycles across the street.

"Watch for cars, gentlemen!"

And when all the players were beyond ear shot, "Notice all the players showed – and early."

"You're not surprised are you?"

"No. Not really."

At T.J, some of the players talked and knew each other from their respective schools and, of course, from playing with or against each other during the season. It was immediately noted Casey Urzak might take over the position as the smallest player on the team from "Kuiper" but it was close. He was quick and played centerfield on the Yankees. Urzak was the only player at the tryout who did not play the infield and Stephen Marsch was one of the few who had not played shortstop all season – besides fulltime catchers like Bob Shuman and first baseman and pitchers like Jay "Noose" Nusman. Stephen Marsch did pitch some innings and played first and third base for the powerhouse Athletics. And the players figured out, themselves, the Cardinals and Pirates were the only National League teams not to have a representative; the Senators and Tigers not representing the American League. Of the sixteen teams, twelve were represented at the tryout.

Coach Sherwin – the manager of the Red Sox – certainly did not have a problem with this, although, to the players he was a quiet coach and it may have been difficult to tell if anything – or everything – bothered him. Even his player, Harrison "Harry" Dodd, had a difficult time reading his manager. Coach Sherwin did not smile much behind his thick, black, Fu Manchu-like mustache.

Harrison Dodd wore his team's dark blue jersey with red trim on the sleeves and numbers. Michael Blake waited for a coach to speak directly to him, probably feeling more comfortable if Coach Donald from the Orioles had been there, while Tim Lake from the White Sox quietly stood by. The Indians Sam Brocco, chewing on some bubble gum and wearing his red team jersey with the white lettering, did the same.

Coach Manta was coaxed by Mr. Mason to hit a "hard" infield practice. "I want to see who's afraid of the ball."

The coaches wore their Manager's league baseball hat – Mr. Mason the Athletics, Mr. Manta the Phillies, and Mr. Sherwin the Red Sox – displaying the Insignia or Letter of the team name on the front of their hats; Mr. Mason's "A's" spelled out with the apostrophe and the small *s* in its abbreviated entirety; the white *P* on Coach Manta's purplish hat; and one red sock on Coach Sherwin's hat appearing slightly like a kids red hockey stick or a fat letter L, from a distance.

"Everyone out to shortstop...!" Mr. Mason called-out as he sat behind the fence, in the dugout-bench on the third base side.

And Coach Manta hit as many hard grounders and choppers that he could, pretending not to feel the need to let Mr. Sherwin hit in his place. He felt his round belly that, pretty much, all three coaches had absorbed since hitting their mid-forties.

As the grounders progressed and the line rotated, the usual players became more enthusiastic as a few players, nervously, bobbled, missed, or made a few too many off-the-mark throws to Coach Sherwin.

Shortstops Tommy Lotts and T.C – who both played for Mr. Charles and the Dodgers – started pushing each other not to miss and "show some range" as Mr. Manta began moving the fielders towards second and then the next fielder to the "hole" at short to test the backhand. These two along with Dan Grossman, "Kuiper", and to an extent, "Noose" Nusman and Kenney Richmond were good, confident infielders, even if they did not show quite the enthusiasm of the Dodgers rotating shortstops, or Grossman and Kuiper. Noose recalled that he had played third base for a few games as a 10-year-old but had not played their sense. He was left-handed so the inevitable move landed him at first base, regularly, when he was not pitching. And "Harry" Dodd instinctively displayed his infield reflexes as well as the ability to play multiple positions. Add that to the chemistry-jell mixing with the two "other" players from the Athletics – Bart "Garvey" and Stephen Marsch – diving for groundballs in practice and the intensity began to pick-up to the delight of the three coaches.

"Great effort...! Keep it in front, that's it!" Coach Mason encouraged from the bench.

"Nobody get hurt out there," Mr. Manta paused to breathe and remind the players. "We have a lot of games to play still. Don't throw your arms out...easy on the throws... just get them to Coach Sherwin."

T.C fired his last quick snap, overhand strike to the coach.

"Hey Kuiper," the ball skipped and bounced, upward, off of the second-baseman's left arm, "you missed one...must be the glasses."

"That took a wicked hop," he answered rubbing his 12-year-old bicep, quickly, asking for another grounder. He had kept it in front of him. There was a pride of a groundball within reach not getting behind the fielder.

"Everyone can catch the easy one's," George Dakalos heckled from the line of players behind the fielder.

Another skipping three-hopper came and this ball stayed down as did the Red Legs representative on his right knee, back-handing the ball and, in one rising, three-quarters motion, let the throw rise and drop easily to Mr. Sherwin.

"Smooth..." came the call from behind.

"That's you...Duane Hoover!"

"What...?" It was new to everybody in the line except to T.C and Tommy Lotts who, apparently, had been working on the nickname extension. Tommy Lotts explained:

"Like the Hoover vacuum cleaner...he sucks-up everything...he's still like Duane Kuiper with the glove."

The players hesitated and smiled thinking about it.

"Hey, Top Cat thought of it, not me." This was the reason T.C had – what was beginning to seem like forever to him – been responding to the initials by name. It had begun from the Hanna-Barbara *Top Cat* cartoon that aired non-stop for about a year on the WUAB Channel 43 network broadcast in Lorain and Cleveland. Once the elementary school kids had seen the show and heard the theme song "...Top Cat, the indisputable leader of the gang..." it was over, in a sense. The initials stuck like the permanence of his last name, Charles. And, actually, T.C got the first initial from his middle name, when his younger sister had let the T.C "cat" out of the bag. But all's fair when a nickname is being born. But, T.C could hit, pitch, run and was destined to be a starter, again, for Euclid's All-Star team. And being the "Top Cat" was not such a bad moniker for a 12-year-old preparing to improve and help be an example of how to win more baseball games. His dad had said, "... If you make fewer mistakes than the other team, you'll win. And if you don't win, the better team won and that's nothing to be ashamed of."

And the Charles siblings would kid their dad, "Okay, Mr. Brady," for sounding like the paternal lecturer from the 70's T.V show.

And the players like T.C and Noose were beginning to see these tournaments as a great learning experience for junior high school where the competition should continue to improve their own game. Their improvement could seem, respectfully, limitless. There was no telling how good they or someone else like the, already, stocky Kenney Richmond could become. Adults were already saying he had the legs and thighs of a football running back. The thought of the first days of junior high school probably were not as nervous for players like T.C, Noose, or Richmond but, more than likely, they were – if they did not show it.

"Oh. Got it Top Cat...!"

"You dog...!"

And the rotation continued:

"Nice play Bart."

"Good job Gross."

"That's why Tommy's the shortstop."

"Damn Hoover." And everybody stopped. "Hoover Dam...!" And they laughed.

And a ball glanced low off the leg of George Dakalos.

"Ah, man, my shin splints!"

And Coach Mason could not control a snicker.

"You alright...?"

"Yeah, I'm alright."

"Your hair looks good still," Coach Sherwin could not help but tease, almost smiling.

"Thanks," Dakalos said, sarcastically, replacing the blue Braves hat atop his long, thick black hair. He took another ground ball and went to the back of the line with a slight limp.

The dusty haired Sam Brocco wiped some sweat off his brow with the underside of his short-sleeved, red Indians shirt and proceeded to charge a ball and field it on one big hop. "That was easy." And he lobbed the ball to Coach Sherwin.

"Do you want another?"

"How can I say no?"

And Coach Manta drilled a low "screamer" that was diffi-cult to tell if it would contact the infield dirt before reaching Brocco who froze as the ball whizzed toward his glove side. He "side-saddled" the passing line drive as it short hopped in front of his glove, hit off the heel, and shot high into the air, resembling an infield pop-up. Everybody watched as the ball began its descent, slowly succumbing to the gravity of the situation.

"Mine," Brocco re-called as he moved about six-feet to his left and caught the ball out of the air with a slight lunge, followed by a chuckle.

"Should have called a fair catch," Stephen Marsch said, exaggerating the height and the sport.

"That ball was smoked," Brocco acknowledged as he lobbed the ball in.

"Okay, we're going to take a quick round of batting practice. We don't want to be here all day, okay. Ten swings. Not just one more. And just swing the bats. Every pitch does not have to be perfect. We know you can be more selective in a game. We just want to see you guys swing and make good contact. Okay. Let's do it. Coach Sherwin is going to throw as many strikes as he can. It's just batting practice so he's not going to be throwing any junk at you."

"Well, not too much. My stuff's not as good as it used to be."

The players had never heard Mr. Sherwin talk when they were the opponent. He hardly ever said a thing during the game unless it was to argue with an umpire. And that was not an uncommon occurrence come game day. And, now, that they were on the same side it, suddenly, seemed like they knew him.

Batting practice went quickly. Everybody backed-up for Noose as he almost sent a ball landing into the police station backyard on a fly, just missing the bushes.

Kenney Richmond swung violently and hit line drives that nobody could stop from rolling towards Thomas Jefferson School.

Grossman, T.C, and George Dakalos all pulled the ball well, beating the left fielder three to four times, total, admiring the distance as Urzak or Brocco retrieved the ball, jogging towards the school.

Everyone made contact, a few popped-up, and fewer swung and missed on three consecutive pitches.

When Bart "Garvey" came to the plate everybody watched why and how he got his nickname. His batting stance was the copy of Los Angeles Dodgers first baseman and multiple All-Star, Steve Garvey. Affectionately dubbed "Mr. Clean" by the L.A media for his clean living and family first persona, Steve Garvey played in a National League record 1207 straight games, won four straight gold gloves from 1974-1977, and collected 200 hits in a season six times. Ten times he was an All-Star. He played eight years with the same teammates: shortstop Bill Russell, 3rd baseman Ron "the Penguin" Cey and 2nd baseman Davey Lopes (and catcher Steve Yeager) winning a World Series in 1981. He, also, with his best years supposedly behind him, had one more playoff run with the San Diego Padres helping them reach the postseason for the first time in that franchise's history, hitting a ninth-inning, game ending homerun to help win the National League Pennant against the "cursed" Chicago Cubs in 1984. He ended his career with a .294 batting average and hit all but two of his 272 homeruns from 1971-1986. He concluded his career with just over twenty-five hundred hits, induction into Cooperstown's Baseball Hall of Fame a deserving formality.

In 1979 Steve Garvey and his Dodger teammates were in the prime of – what would become – four World Series appearances. And, supposedly, as Bart said, he was not imitating him. It was just the way he stood at the plate, totally upright; stance slightly closed; his form squared, 90 degrees and angles; left elbow away from his mid-section; the right elbow up and straight; left foot slightly closer to the plate than the right, which pivoted on the ball of its foot, in the dirt; a slight wiggle of the barrel as he set for the pitch and swung the bat level, hands inside the ball, and hitting one high toward center that Sam Brocco was able to run-down, playing deep. Casey Urzak laughed.

"They're not beating us deep again…!" And nobody did. Only a couple of "bloops" would drop in front of them the rest of the practice.

"That's you Garvey. That's to the fence at Vet's." And Noose smiled at his Athletics teammate, surprised how some people did not regard Bart "Garvey" a premier player in Euclid Boy's League. He had been on the 10-year-old All-Star team, too. And he was, still, always the third player mentioned after Jay Nusman and Kenney Richmond. Bart was the everyday shortstop on the A's, the position regularly given to the best all-around player on little league teams. The general disregard for his ability may have stemmed from Bart's quiet, humble demeanor. He never bragged or gloated or, really, ever lost his temper. He, also, did not pitch very often, which was, somewhat unusual for a player of high quality, little league standard. Occasionally, Bart just seemed to take his quiet frustration – if he had any – out on the ball; a 12-year-old image of "Mr. Clean" in rubber cleats, chewing on his bubble-yum.

"Don't like the grape," Bart said, "turns my mouth purple."

The tryout-practice wound down, a few minutes passed two hours. Parents began to drive their cars down E. 262nd Street next to the field and the school. Some walked to the field to watch the end of the practice.

"Okay, men, we're done for the day. We've been out here long enough and your parents are here." Mr. Manta was relieved he had made it through the infield practice without asking anyone to take some swings. He was sweating as much, if not more, than everyone. Mr. Mason told the players, who had congregated in front of the fence by the third base dugout, that they would be in contact and they had to cut the roster to 15.

"We'll call and let you know. Thanks for coming."

"Good luck the rest of the season, boys," Coach Manta added. "We'll see you later."

And the players walked to their parents' cars. The players waved to each other and the coaches and – in a way, it seemed – to the field as they departed, the summer nowhere near over.

A 'CRACKER OF AN INVITATION AND THE 'ATHLETIC' CONTROVERSY

❧

The first game in the Fourth of July, Firecracker Invitational, basically, went as planned. The opponent was from the east side of Cleveland: Lake County's Willowick B team. The most difficult part of the game was convincing Michael Blake he was pitching and there was no need to be nervous. He visibly shook, almost needing help hooking his blue belt through the loops of his white pants. Most of the players found navy blue belts to wear with their red jerseys and the sky blue hats. The reaction had been wide eyed by most when the uniforms were, first, revealed. They were colorful and, certainly, did not lack originality. The white sleeves (with thin red pin-stripes to boot) almost seemed like a separate part of a sleeveless red jersey. But, it was all one shirt. The idea of not having a solid colored jersey was quite unique for the players, and the parents, in 1979.

"Who thought of these?" was asked more than once, not too critically. The uniforms were patriotic and never easy to ignore.

But, this was the least of Michael Blake's worries. He aimed and prayed to get through the first inning.

He walked the bases loaded and, it was apparent, the second team from Willowick was not going to swing until Blake proved he could consistently throw strikes. One opponent swung at a 3-2 pitch and missed for one of his two strikeouts in the inning. Grossman – who had worked in a league game just to prepare as a catcher for the All-Star team – was berating himself for letting a fastball, barely in the dirt, bounce passed his backhand allowing a run to score. The coaches did not have to say a word to him. He knew. Get in front of the ball!

Euclid rallied and scored four in the bottom half of the inning on two doubles and two walks and two passed balls. Euclid's confidence soared as they knew they should dismiss the opponent by a run-rule while showing no disrespect. They just *should* and were capable of ending the game early. And, in a tournament, saving a pitcher's innings for later in the week, if needed, could be crucial.

Michael Blake, then, walked the bases loaded again with one out and Coach Mason had to take a trip to the 6-inch "bump" to calm his pitcher.

"I'd rather see them hit the ball. Hey, relax...! These guys want some action out here. Any base...! There's a force every-where!" He called to his infielders.

And right on cue a groundball was hit at Euclid's second baseman. "Kuiper" charged and fielded the groundball just as the runner passed in front of him. In the same motion, moving forward, Euclid's second baseman grabbed the ball from the dirt, slapped a tag on the hip of the base runner – who tried to avoid him, running inside the baseline – flipping a submarine throw to first, and rolling on the infield dirt as the field umpire ruled "Out" twice, ending the inning. Blake, smiling, immediately patted his successful defender on the back as he got to his feet, and the entire team jogged off the field, vocal, as they approached their first base dugout. They took turns stepping through the doorway in the dugout fence clapping with each other to score more runs.

Euclid's players, cheering for each batter, proceeded to score three more runs in the bottom of the 2nd and the comfortable win was well underway. They led 7-1 after two-innings and Michael Blake settled in. More and more his pitches began to slice the outside corners, dipping across the knee strike zone to the opponent's stock of right-handed batters. The strikeouts mounted, the pop-ups and slow grounders limited and routine, and by of 6th inning Blake was throwing a no-hitter with Euclid leading 10-1.

In the top of the sixth Blake seemed to tire, loading the bases on two walks and a hit batsman. But, he still had a no-hitter! And, after a brief discussion between back-up catcher

Shuman and pitcher Blake, he responded by striking out the next hitter on a straight change-up, the hitter corkscrewing himself in the batter's box.

Blake then pounded two more knee high strikes to the next hitter before another groundball was rolled to shortstop, Tommy Lotts flipping the ball to his second baseman to end the inning.

The run-rule game ended in style when Richmond pulled a three-run homer over the Veteran's Field left field fence, closing the scorebook on the game at 13-1. "Noose" – starting at first-base – also hit a two-run homer, earlier in the game, over the 220 ft. sign in right-field. Michael Blake completed his first All-Star game by striking out 11 and walking 8 in the 6-inning complete game victory, causing some to joke "he must have thrown 150 pitches in the process," no doubt more than a slight exaggeration. He had not allowed a base runner in the 3rd and 4th-innings.

And Euclid's young All-Stars waited to hear who they would play in their second game, remembering the play of a potential opponent as 10-year-olds in the same 4th of July Tournament.

"Bee-Buzz...? The team from Warrensville or E. Cleveland...? They didn't beat Maple Heights, did they...?"

"They're still playing at T.J."

"We crushed B-Buzz two years ago..."

"No. I just heard Coach Mason saying the game went seven...we're playing Maple Heights."

"They should be good."

"Maple Heights won," Coach Mason conferred, returning from the game's final pitch from across the street.

T.C was slated to start the next game.

Two days later he did.

Again, Euclid would score early and often but, in the 3rd inning Maple Heights strung together three straight hits from the top of their order to end the shutout and cut the deficit in half, 6-3. Maple's second pitcher would keep them in the game.

Dan Grossman, Bart "Garvey", playing left field, and Sam Brocco, starting in right, all had RBI hits to compliment the middle-of-the-order bashers, led by Richmond, adding two, two RBI, extra base hits. T.C added a multi-hit game including a triple and two runs scored to help his cause. Grossman pitched the last two innings. The final: 7-4.

Euclid's 12-year-olds awaited their next opponent. They knew it would get tougher. And it might have been Euclid's B team, who was playing across the street at T.J at the same time. They were confident and wanted to play the "A" team for obvious reasons. They, certainly, had something to prove.

"They couldn't pull it off," the news, again, arrived from across the street. "Lost 7-2..." Parents from both the A and B teams had spent time walking back and forth to compare scores.

The next opponent would be Mentor. Located in Lake County Mentor was regarded the largest suburb in the area and, it seemed, always competitive no matter what sport, age, or sex. It was also basically regaled that the Mentor community was one of high standard and money. There was little to believe they would not be competitive. They had won two games to get to the semi-final. And Coach Manta had done his homework, too, watching Mentor's victory played on the afternoon after Euclid's win over Willowick B.

"They've got some good pitching and they were watching us play too," Coach Manta said of Mentor. "They've been scouting us."

Jay Nusman was scheduled to pitch the third game. Euclid's coaches did not want to dwell-on the fact that their ace pitcher would get them passed their opponent, at risk of jinxing or influencing their young players to plan ahead and not take care of the task at hand.

"One at a time, boys," Coach Manta reminded. "One batter, one inning, one game...! We still have to score more than the other team."

Euclid's players looked at each other in response to the obvious statement but knew what their coaches meant: They could not afford to be over confident.

And, again, Euclid's #1 pitcher showed why he was just that. The game went almost effortlessly, and surprisingly easy, as "Noose" struck out 13, gave up just two hits and hit another fence clearing homerun. The final was 6-1 as Coach Mason watched his other star Athletic, Kenney Richmond, hit another RBI double. With Noose pitching Michael Blake showed his value by filling in at first base and connecting on two doubles himself. He was far from a nervous fluke.

Euclid was in the Final. Their opponent: South Euclid.

An immediate rivalry had been born, with both teams sharing bragging rights for the same city name: One, north, and located on the Lake Erie shoreline; the other inland, south, and smaller in population. Actually, the rivalry had existed for years, in a sense, their high school football teams meeting as early as 1926: Euclid Central High School beating South High School, 50-0!

Euclid was founded in 1797, just one year after Moses Cleaveland had begun his mapping of Cleveland, and covered 35 sq. miles before succumbing in size to some of the other towns and "villes" in the area (there was a Euclidville until Lyndhurst would develop on its own and change its name). Euclid would build its first high school in 1894 (on what would become North Street and is now Euclid's Historical Museum) and close in 1912 to build two separate high schools: Euclid Central High School and Shore High School. These two Euclid high schools would play an annual football game against each other from 1924 until 1949 – when Euclid High School on E. 222nd Street was opened and became the only high school in Euclid.

South Euclid would have its first high school built in 1912 and officially became its own city in 1917.

In 1978, South Euclid had won the previous years Firecracker Invitational from its host and lakeside neighbor. It was time to bring the trophy north.

The championship game was played on July 8th, 1979. And, since this was the championship game, the host team was not designated the home team, which was decided by a simple coin toss. South Euclid won the toss and, naturally, chose to be the home team to receive last at-bats.

A few more "fans" than usual appeared including a small circle of teenage girls who, apparently, were acquaintances of George Dakalos and his thick, black locks.

"Gees, isn't that one girl going in the ninth-grade?"

"I'm not sure," even Dakalos had responded, smiling some, "I think she is. I know the one better."

"Keep your head in the game boys," Coach Mason reminded.

It did not matter which girl Dakalos, actually, knew. Older girls had come to watch them play. This could be good for their junior high school reputations. If just for a day, Dakalos was christened the "Greek God."

There was no score until the fourth inning when a lead-off walk proved as costly as the old baseball adage states. A rare throwing error by Euclid's catcher sent the base-on-balls runner to third, who, then, scored on a ground ball. And, after a base hit and an out, South Euclid's four-hitter roped a fastball over the left-center field fence at least 250 ft. away. Nobody had seen a ball hit like that off Euclid pitching in the tournament. Suddenly, Euclid trailed their rival, southern neighbor, 3-0.

The momentum had obviously shifted. South Euclid's substitutes seemed to be contributing more than Euclid's subs. The base hit before the crushing home run came on a South Euclid reserves first at-bat of the game.

"That's okay. We still have six outs to go."

Euclid would not remain shutout for long.

South Euclid's pitcher appeared to be tiring by the sixth inning. He gave up a lead-off single to Dan Grossman. Then,

Sam Brocco scorched a ball to right field that the outfielder scooped cleanly and in one motion fired a throw that beat Grossman on the close force play at second base. Euclid was stunned while South celebrated another, apparent, momentum changing out. A fresh arm was sent into the game by South's manager to preserve the momentum and the game. He did not seem to throw as hard but appeared to be deceptive in his fluid wind-up and motion.

There was one out and one on in the top of the sixth when T.C stepped to the plate. He looked at the first pitch for ball one. T.C was confident and due for a clutch hit in tournament play. He told his teammates before stepping to the plate he was due. The second pitcher did not throw as hard. The ball came...And it was just a matter if it would stay fair or not down the left field line. The ball cleared the 210 ft. sign, pulling Euclid within one run.

But, South Euclid came right back with a shot almost an exact duplicate of Euclid's two-run homer in the top half of the inning, clearing the fence and hooking late into foul territory over 210 ft. away. With two outs and another runner on base Coach Mason removed Grossman and T.C retired the last batter of the inning.

South led 4-2 to start the 7th-inning just three outs away from defending their 4th of July title. Euclid started the rally with back to back doubles by Michael Blake – his third of the tournament – and Bart "Garvey" cutting the lead to one.

South's reliever tried to remove the sweat from his forehead with his jersey sleeve.

Bob Shuman's walk was sandwiched between two outs. One of Euclid's reserves, Stephen Marsch – the fourth of the Athletics on the squad – was called to bat by Coach Mason. He had batted three times in the previous three games and was hitless.

"Stephen, after you hit you're going in right-field...got it!" Coach Mason boldly stated like a prophet.

Marsch nodded and took a few more practice swings before entering the batters box. Everybody knew this was the ballgame. If Stephen Marsch did not get on base like Coach Mason predicted, the game was over. There would be no right field for anyone.

The count dragged on as Stephen Marsch fouled-off a good fastball and then a slow curve. The count was 2-2.

"Way to battle!"

Then South Euclid's reliever uncorked a wild pitch that had "Garvey" departing for third base as soon as the ball hit the dirt. He knew there would be no chance of the catcher fielding the ball cleanly. Shuman, watching his teammate, followed sliding into second base without a throw.

And, on the next pitch, Marsch sent a fastball back through the box that bounced by second base and into center-field. "Garvey" back-pedaled to home plate, waving his arm for Shuman to do the same. Coach Manta moved down the third base line and wind-milled his left arm, spiraling, faster and faster. Shuman did not hesitate. South Euclid's center-fielder threw the ball up the first base line and Euclid had the go ahead run without a tag. The score: 5-4! When the dust cleared at the plate there were a collection of fist pumps and the calls and points were directed at Marsch who stood at first base receiving a quick handshake and a pat-on-the-back from Coach Sherwin. They both tried not to smile, much, but it was practically impossible, especially for the 12-year-old.

But the game was not over. Behind the first base dugout, Coach Mason's spoke to his other Athletic fireball pitcher, Kenney Richmond, about pitching the seventh inning to preserve the win.

"Are you sure, coach?" Kenney had said. "You don't want to stick with T.C?"

"T.C...?"

"I'm fine," T.C said, putting on his batting helmet, a chance to hit again.

"Okay, go help your cause."

"C'mon, just a base hit...we need more."

"One's not enough."

T.C knocked the doughnut off his bat and kicked the 4 oz. cylinder and some dirt toward the dugout entrance. He walked to the plate, stepped into the batter's box, and did not wait for the second pitch.

And he did it again. This time the ball skipped off the bar atop the left-field fence – and over – for a 7-4 lead! The ball lay in the grass, not much further from the previous homerun he had hit, waiting to be retrieved short of Tungsten Avenue. Euclid's bench laughed and T.C did, also; but shortening his celebration upon remembering he still had to pitch the bottom-of-the-seventh.

"Whew, we got some breathing room."

"Let's finish this off, now."

When the inning ended Coach Manta opened his mouth as if to say something, but did not. It was too late to second guess. T.C was pitching as Tommy Lotts went to the bench and the versatile Harry Dodd put some time in at second base. In right field was the hero at the moment, Stephen Marsch. Bart "Garvey" remained in the game at shortstop.

A collective groan permeated from Euclid's side of the field when T.C walked the first batter. Parents along the fence on the first base line turned their backs to the field before collecting themselves to continue watching.

"We still got a game to finish let's go!" Coach Manta pleaded, somewhat out of character.

And T.C regained control. His short stride and extreme, overhand motion that ended with his arm extending in an upside-down C was quick to the plate. He seemed to jump at the hitter with his short stride. The strikes and outs arrived on top of each other.

There were two outs.

"Just one more..."

And T.C pounded the strike zone. And South Euclid began to hit the ball, again. First, a solid base hit pulled to left was followed by a swinging bunt that could not be fielded before all base runners arrived safely. The bases were loaded.

All the players stood in their bench areas, hands in their respective dugout fences. Mothers laughed and said they could not watch. The tying run was on base!

Another base hit found a hole and two runs scored: the score was 7-6! The only thing going in Euclid's favor – besides the score – was the fact the middle of South Euclid's order was not batting. But, still, the South reserves were hitting! Now, it was the top-of-the-order. It certainly would not be as simple as throwing strikes which had not worked for the last three hitters anyways.

T.C threw a curveball on the first pitch: ball one.

The hitter dug-in. The pitch came and the fastball was a strike and rerouted, over the infield, toward right field.

T.C turned to watch the path of the looping line drive sinking toward the foul line. "Oh no," could be read from his lips as he turned to watch the path of the ball.

Stephen Marsch, the hero "for the moment" in the seventh inning with the two out, base hit, ran in and towards the right field foul line, reaching with his glove, sliding feet first, grass-staining his white pants while kicking chalk into the air. The runner from second base would score easily if the ball was not caught, tying the game. If the ball skipped passed Euclid's right fielder the runner from first would, more than likely, score ending the game.

Stephen Marsch popped-up to his feet showing the ball securely placed in the web of his glove.

South Euclid yelled in protest, "Trap," but their argument did not last long.

The field umpire made the call and Mr. Mason was the first on the field, literally, placing the 12-year-old Athletic on his shoulders to parade him off the field; Coach Mason, as the human float, carrying the honoree he had always had faith in. Euclid's players rejoiced at the enthusiasm of their manager-coach running to his side to slap hands with Stephen from below as they exhaled in minor disbelief, themselves, how the game had prevailed in their favor.

"Okay, young man, you're heavier than I thought," and Coach Mason set Stephen down, two feet back on the ground, as he received more pats on the back and smiles from his teammates.

Mr. Manta looked at Mr. Charles who stood behind the dugout, smiling, only the fence between father and coach; team and son; the fathers prideful and realizing how special Euclid's young All-Stars were becoming.

Mr. Charles and Mr. Billups would be the coaches for the Willoughby Hills tournament. Mr. Manta would be there, again, also.

Mr. Billups sat in the stands with his wife and 11-year-old son who played for his dad on the Cubs. They clapped together, briefly, and observed the small, jubilant herd along the first base dugout.

Mr. Billups listened. There was another tournament to be played and there was definitely excitement in the air.

"I hope their luck's not running out now that I'm gonna' be coaching," Coach Billups said to his son, Walter.

"After a win like that they gotta' be feeling good about themselves."

"Think you might watch them – us – in Willoughby?" Mr. Billups asked his son.

"Yeah, I don't see why not. I'm sure mom will go too."
Walter watched some of the attentive "All-Star" parents. Mrs.
Richmond and Mrs. Charles hugged, while Mr. Richmond
and Mr. Nusman talked and laughed amongst them selves,
shaking their heads in some disbelief. And the Dodd's and
the Pembroke's – who lived on the same Euclid, 207 Street –
stood by and briefly recollected what they had just witnessed.

The younger sisters of T.C and Stephen Marsch stood by
the right field fence in foul territory. Sally Marsch laughed
and called her older brother lucky.

And Walter Billups enjoyed what he saw. He knew this
could be him next year, celebrating 12-year-old, All-Star
victories – as well as a possible Cubs championship or two.

"See you next time!?"

"Think they can do it again...?" The parents would seem to
have some doubt, but no one disagreed. At least not out loud.

THE SHOT HEARD 'ROUND WILLOUGHBY HILLS

❧

The tournament in Willoughby Hills was very similar to Euclid's Firecracker Invitational. Mentor and Willowick would be present – two teams Euclid defeated in their 4th of July tournament. Also, arriving in Willoughby Hills Park, not far from the three blocks of businesses that constituted "downtown" Willoughby, were Bedford, Mayfield, Maple Heights and Garfield Heights – located in Cuyahoga County – as well as Euclid.

Bedford was not known for being competitive, at the time. But, Garfield Heights was expected to challenge for another title, having hosted the longest running tournament in the area while contending for multiple Boys League tournament titles, yearly. Mayfield was, also, known for being competitive and hosting the 10-year-old baseball tournament. Maple

Heights seemed to loom over Euclid's shoulders after the reasonably close 7-4 game played in the Firecracker Invitational.

Coach Mason informed Coaches Billups and Manta that they would have a roster spot to fill since Michael Blake had not been exaggerating about leaving with his parents "later in the summer."

"Apparently," Mr. Mason said, "his father might have to move again because of work. Michael won't be available for the tournament."

"Should we find another pitcher?"

"We should find a position player not averse to sitting," Coach Charles said.

After seeing the twenty-one selections the sixteen coaches had selected on their ten-player ballots, Mr. Billups, agreeing with Coach Charles, thought he knew who the player should be. Coach Billups had his Cubs playing well despite a roster full of 11-year-olds contributing key roles. And that had been an important part of the Cubs surprise success. Each player understood their role on the team. They were not succeeding with "star" players. They were playing together and doing what they were asked. They were bunting and hitting their cut-off men and limiting their opponent's extra outs. There was no complaining about playing time. The best players were starting and everyone knew who they were. His 11-year-old son, Walter, was the third pitcher and played three infield positions.

The All-Star team needed a utility player and Coach Billups would be fair and suggest somebody deserving from the Managers' ballot list. There were no other 12-year-olds on the list from the Cubs, which he understood, and chose the player he thought would best "fit-in" with the team.

"We should just take the kid from the Yankees who played centerfield every game. He'll play any outfield position and he'll be happy to play when the time comes. We could use him as a pinch runner. He's got a good glove too."

"Okay. I know who you mean," Coach Manta quickly agreed.

A small convoy of cars left for Willoughby Hills, some of the players hitching rides with other parents. It was not unusual for two players to ride in the same car with a coach or another player's parents.

"Okay, Cole, don't drive me crazy," Coach Billups said.

"I won't," Cole Pembroke said, sincerely, not wanting to aggravate his Cubs manager.

"It's only a fifteen minute drive, right dad?"

"That's right, Walt."

"We should survive," Mr. Billups son predicted.

"I'm glad you think so...but will we win."

"Of course as long as Noose is pitching...!"

Cole Pembroke did not say anything.

"He can't pitch every game," Coach Billups reminded his son.

"This is very true."

"Cole, you think you might be ready for a game?"

"I don't know. I only started pitching this year, really..."

"Well, we'll see," Coach Billups said. "We'll know soon enough."

"Mom said she was coming in the other car later, right?"

"Oh, yeah, she'll be there. She's bringing the water cooler. And she said she might pick-up some of that Gator Gum everyone seems to be chewing."

The parents would, also, take turns driving depending on work schedules or just plain old fatigue from driving every two days to a suburb across the county. But, more and more, as the traveling tournaments progressed and the victories mounted, pretty much every parent who had a son on the All-Star team would make the next game if there was absolutely nothing – especially work related – to prevent them from attending.

It is, really, not that amazing what winning can do. It nurtures confidence and calms the soul. It can help cure a foul mood and prevent moral dilemmas; camaraderie slipping into a wondrously patented comfort zone.

"You guys won again?"

"Yes, we beat'em easy..."

"I'll be at the next game, son. I'll tell work what I'm doing. They should understand."

"Sweet...!"

And a drive in a car might go something like this, when all is well:

"You've seen that Bugs Bunny cartoon when Bugs is making fools of the mobsters...?"

"Yeah, yeah," and to the 12-year-olds who had seen the cartoon-short about five times each, the laughing rose ahead of the actual story or punch line. And the parent or coach in the front seat, driving their prospects, could generally relate since they had, more than likely, seen the cartoon, too, since the Warner Bros. animation being discussed had its origins in the 1950's, when most of the parents were in their youth, also.

And the lines would be remembered and imitated.

"...Clancy, take the boys and surround the house," complete with a 12-year-old faking an Irish brogue.

And: "...Hide me rabbit..." the mobster portrayed sounding stupid beyond belief, "duh, hide me too...please bunny hide me too."

And Bugs Bunny looks at the camera: "It can't be dis easy..."

And he hides the gangsters in the oven.

"Would I t'row a lighted match into the oven if my friend Mugsy were in there?"

"Eh, you might rabbit you might," the Irish brogue says, again, and even the driver of the car is chuckling at this point.

Boom! The oven expands and jumps and bursts spewing black smoke. But, the oven door never opens!

"Okay, rabbit." And Clancy and the Irish cops leave quicker than they arrived, sirens blaring.

"Oh, man, a classic!"

"Well, actually, Bugs was pretending to be the cops and, then, they really do arrive, repeating, word for word, what Bugs had already said, right down to the oven exploding again and the mobsters give themselves up to the cops because they can't take it anymore."

"Yep, that's right. And Bugs is promoted to Detective or something by the end for helping capture the mobsters..."

"Right, right...do that again."

"It can't be dis easy..."

"Clancy, take the boys and surround..."

And they laughed, some more, without it being necessary to repeat the line in its entirety.

"Hey, coach, we need to pick-up some of that Gator Gum... we don't want to mess with a winning streak..."

"Are you serious...?" The coaches wondered not wanting to mess with a baseball superstition.

As the Willoughby Hills tournament progressed, Euclid had little trouble disposing of Mentor and Willowick B, again, scoring 15 runs on sixteen hits against one and scoring twenty runs in a five-inning run-rule that included homeruns by "Harry" Dodd, Bart "Garvey", and Kenney Richmond against Willowick's outmanned, second unit. "Noose", again, had double-digit strikeouts in his complete game victory.

Despite the easy wins there were some developing concerns. Tommy Lotts, for one, had slipped into a mild, mental and physical, shortstop slump. He had no hits in the previous three games and was officially 0 for his last nine at-bats and did not appear as aggressive in the field after a throwing error.

Dan Grossman, now their proven catcher, also, was in a slump having zero hits in his last seven at-bats. The thought from the coaches was starting and catching every game was taking its toll on Grossman. He was tired, not concentrating as much and becoming impatient at the plate. The coaches noted every at-bat Grossman seemed to be "way out in front of the ball" and, when he made contact, he was on his front foot.

The coaches began to work with him and a "timing mechanism" to keep his hands back as the pitcher began his wind-up before the delivery to the plate. The plan was to get Grossman to rotate his torso and hands back from his stomach as the pitcher began his wind-up. The reasoning was to get Grossman to concentrate on keeping his hands back while, also, keeping them lower than his shoulders. He looked robotic but his hands and bat were not moving as much – and, definitely, not moving forward until the pitch arrived.

Coach Charles then had Grossman sit for the start of the semi-final – as did Tommy Lotts. They were a bit stunned, but they understood.

"Just take it easy guys," Coach Billups told them, "we're gonna' need you before this is all over. You guys have contributed too much too fail us now."

And they nodded and waited for their chance to contribute.

After pitching game #1 "Noose" was scheduled to throw in game #3 (the semi). Euclid felt reasonably prepared to be playing on the same field they had played the previous games, although, this time the game would be played under lights in Willoughby, Ohio. Playing under the lights was not completely foreign to them. Most of them had played under lights in the Mayfield championship game when they were ten.

Euclid, however, would not be quite prepared for Garfield's pitcher.

A story quickly spread that the Garfield pitcher was a young relative of the one-and-only track and Olympic star Jesse Owens who had attended Ohio State and had relatives in Northeast Ohio! Was it true? If it was not true the young man pitched as well as the impressive and intimidating bloodline.

"Kuiper" led-off for the second straight game. The pitcher for Garfield Heights was as good as they had seen – especially his curveball which complimented his fastball immensely; the spots he seemed to hit on demand. After Euclid's second baseman tapped back to the mound everybody waited for his reply.

"Yes, he has a curveball...and it's good."

Game after game, in the tournaments, Euclid had grown accustomed to watching the other side strikeout 12-13 times when "Noose" was pitching; placing a "stranglehold" and tightly securing any lead Euclid would gain on the way to victory. This game, quickly, had a different feel. By the third inning Garfield's not too imposing pitcher by appearance – he, really, was not very big or tall – had his curve consistently working as an out pitch.

He was perfect through three innings with six strikeouts.

Then in the fourth Noose walked two batters and a run scored after a wild pitch and a ground out. With two outs and a runner in scoring position Noose jammed a right-handed hitter on a 1-2 pitch and the ball lofted over Harrison Dodd's head at first base and landed just on the grass for a base hit to score the second run of the inning. Dodd shook his head in disgust because the ball could have been kicked harder and farther compared to where it landed just out of his back-to-the-plate reach.

Garfield Heights led 2-0! And Euclid, still, would not have a hit after the fourth inning. Euclid's lead-off hitter connected on a 1-2 pitch, lining it to the left of center, but Garfield's centerfielder was positioned perfectly and caught the ball at his chest while stepping into the gap.

"I don't think he's throwing his curve as much," the second baseman told his coaches and teammates.

"Hang in there, he might be getting tired." The coaches implied and everybody hoped.

In the fifth, Euclid got their first base runner on an unintentional-intentional five pitch walk to Euclid's slugger-pitcher. Jay Nusman would barely see a pitch to hit all game. Garfield's coaches had decided they were not going to let the imposing four-hitter's bat beat them.

But, now the tying run was coming to the plate in the form of Kenney Richmond. He was due...and he struck out on a high fastball for the first out. Euclid's bench quieted, again.

Then, before the next hitter could fall behind in the count, as had been the pattern for the game, Sam Brocco sent a high fly to left-center that seemed to float farther than it did rapidly. The ball carried and rattled the four-foot high fence, shockingly, just below where the 200 ft. sign might read – if one were placed on the fence in left-center. Noose did not have to slide into third, and instantly, there was a renewed life within the Euclid dugout. A couple players shook the fence and some slapped the cement wall behind them with their fielding glove, once and twice, announcing their rejuvenation from the lifeless taste of their deficit. The cement roof suddenly gave them some breathing room. They did not feel as restricted. Brocco clapped his hands and nodded as he stood with one foot on second base.

Catcher Bob Schuman, then, was able to make enough contact, hitting a ground ball behind the runners and Noose scored from third.

Euclid had cut the lead in half, 2-1!

But, they did not get any closer.

And, Euclid went down in the sixth. They were quieting, again. Kuiper did not want to be pinch-hit after hitting the ball hard his previous at-bat.

"I'm on him," Kuiper pleaded.

"Good game...we're gonna' give Pembroke a try."

When Cole Pembroke walked on four pitches it looked like Garfield's pitcher might have finally tired and lost it. But, after a visit to the mound he was back on track and the inning ended innocently. Garfield's pitcher struck out his tenth and the score remained 2-1 heading to the 7th and final inning.

Noose responded, again, and retired Garfield in order.

It was the bottom-of-the-seventh. And Euclid would pinch-hit for Sam Brocco, who had their only hit. He threw his glove against the cement wall and tried to calm himself. He had become more serious as the wins began to pile-up. He spit-out his Gator Gum. Brocco stared at the wadded dirt magnet too late to replace his impulsive action. He had never talked much but now he was having a difficult time controlling his outward frustration, stewing where he sat in the dugout. His hat came off his head and he looked down. He seemed to talk to himself, whispering, "c'mon, c'mon...," hoping he had not released a bad vibe in the process.

Noose led-off the inning. If ever someone could tie the game on one swing, it was their four-hitter. Even a walk to get the tying run on base would be sufficient. Euclid's highest on base percentage did neither. He struck out on a 3-2 pitch swinging, the catcher hanging on to the partially tipped ball.

Kenney Richmond was next and continued to struggle against Garfield's deceptive fastball and curveball pitcher. He seemed to throw a slow-change-curve that had not been witnessed before that Richmond reached for with two strikes and popped-up to the third baseman for two outs.

Euclid was on the other end of escalating noise rising from the first base side of the field. Garfield's pitcher took a deep breath and cracked a smile for the first time.

"One more to go, let's go...!" Garfield's coach reminded.

"Anybody got a fresh stick of Gator Gum?" Tommy Lotts asked from Euclid's third base dugout. There was one orange and green rectangular pack laying on the bench open and ready for the taking.

Tommy Lotts walked through the on-deck circle toward the batter's box for his first at-bat of the game. He appeared to react, somewhat, uncomfortably before stepping into the box. He had never come off the bench before. He paused to chew his stiff piece of gum.

And, he quickly, fell behind in the count 0-2.

From Euclid's bench could be heard desperate, lifeless claps but not much more as the plea, "c'mon" came in whispers.

It was 1-2 when Lotts turned in his wide-stance and smacked the pitch through the middle passed a diving second baseman. Euclid had their second hit of the game.

"All right...!"

"Way to go Tommy...!" He had snapped his 0-9 skid.

Next to the plate, for the first time in the game, was Dan Grossman in the midst of his 0'fer and a "timing mechanism" that had him looking at his Coach at third to remind him of his hands and torso rotation.

And he proceeded to rotate for strike one. Players wondered if he had taken his Gator Gum.

Dan Grossman bent his knees slightly. His stance was closed. He did not swing at the next two pitches as his hands and torso rotated back to remind him to be patient and see the ball.

The count – again – was 1 ball and 2 strikes.

Nobody on Euclid's bench stood. Coach Billups at third clapped his hands. Coach Charles held his scorebook by his side as he watched the next pitch preparing for its final flight to the plate.

Grossman bent in his stance; his hands moved with his torso, back; the ball arrived; and he swung and snapped his wrists through the ball ...and it jumped!...clean and swiftly from his bat!...and every player in the Euclid dugout that had been stuck to the bench leaped from their seats!...and followed the ball!...pushing it as they hooked their hands into the dugout fence!...pushing into the fence!...climbing the fence!... coaxing the ball!...a revelry of synchronized yells...!

"Get outta' here...!"

"Go, go, go...!"

"Get out, get out!"

Tommy Lotts sprinted around second, watching the ball, and yelled thrusting a fist into the air. He knew. Everyone knew as Garfield's centerfielder made an all-out, valiant effort leaving his feet and landing, horizontally, on the fence as the ball cleared the 200 ft sign and the desperate reach of his glove by a few feet.

Coach Charles almost tore his score book throwing his hands in the air to confirm what had happened.

A somber Jay "Noose" Nusman – who had exited the dugout and was by his parents when the ball was struck – reappeared with his mouth agape as Dan Grossman rounded first base, head down, somehow, not showing much emotion.

"He hit it out?" Noose questioned in glorious disbelief.

"Bless that boy...Oh, bless that boy!" Mr. Nusman could be heard, standing behind his son, who was – by this time – on his way back inside the dugout to join the celebration by the side of his teammates.

And Dan Grossman could not help but laugh as he approached third base seeing the pandemonium and jubilation that had erupted from what – just moments before – had been their solemn, third base dugout. The extra time and the timing mechanism had worked with a mathematical precision that seemed quite fitting for a Euclid All-Star. The hitting instructor-coaches felt like geniuses!

Coach Billups slapped Grossman's hand and spun away to watch Euclid's players prepare to mob him at home plate.

"Let him touch the plate!" Coach Manta laughed and called out his eyes not quite as glossy as Jay Nusman's father who could not stand still watching and hearing the celebration growing in volume. The dugout fence shook one last time as Kuiper and Brocco and Urzak finally released from climbing and shaking the fence and were on the field with the remainder of their teammates causing a dust storm of bodies in their jubilant frenzy knocking the sky-blue cap off Dan Grossman's head not once but twice in the process.

"I can't believe what I just saw!" More than one mother said; flooded smiles of joy in just as many of their stunned-in-disbelief faces.

On the field Coach Manta was the first to congratulate the Garfield manager who was hugging his pitcher to help stop a disbelieving and defeated tear from running down his cheek.

"You pitched a great game, son," Coach Manta said. "You didn't deserve to lose." And he rubbed the top of his head as the manager continued to console his pitcher and nodded at Coach Manta as they shook hands. It was then everyone realized the Garfield Manager must have been the pitcher's father – another Owens relation?!

"Thank you."

In centerfield, the outfielder remained laying at the base of the fence. His teammate and left fielder called from his side standing next to him: "Coach, he's hurt...!"

And the Garfield and Euclid coaches ran on the field to the prostrate centerfielder. Both Garfield outfielders and their pitcher kneeled a few feet from their fallen teammate as the coaches immobilized the 12-year-old.

"Don't move him. He said his back hurts."

The outfielder moved his hands.

"That's good. But, don't move anything okay?"

"It's probably bruised but don't move. We're taking no chances."

In the third base dugout Euclid's players head locked Dan Grossman one last time and, slowly, started to file out of the dugout when they realized Garfield's teammate was not getting to his feet.

"I can't believe how he dove over the fence for that ball."

"Did you see it?"

"Yeah, he landed on the top of the fence right on his back. You just don't bend that way."

Mr. Charles and Mr. Billups had backed from Garfield's injured player to let their coaches and his mom and dad remain close to their son. Mr. Manta called the Euclid team to the outfield and, in a long single file of two's, Euclid's All-Stars trekked through the infield through the outfield to congratulate the effort of their injured opponent. One-by-one the hands began to reach down to acknowledge Garfield's outfielder.

"That was a heck of an effort..."

"Thought you had it for a second..."

"Did you have to make it so close...?"

"Nice try, man, you'll be alright."

The Euclid players tapped Garfield's outfielder on the shoulder; or lower on his arm. He responded, on his back, with a slight nod or a lift of his fingers in return.

"Good game," he winced once or twice.

His parents thanked Euclid's players and coaches for their sportsmanship and concern; and the remainder of the Garfield and Euclid teams shook hands on the field – special attention directed towards Garfield's pitcher and his fine pitching performance.

"I can't believe we won...best curve we've seen."

And Garfield's pitcher smiled, eyes, turning upward, not as visibly strained or red.

"Thanks. Congratulations."

Both teams stayed in and around their dugouts until the ambulance arrived about five minutes later. There were a few more cheers when the outfielder was hoisted on the stretcher and into the back of the ambulance.

Grossman received a token paper cup of water over the head as the celebration never completely relinquished.

"Gees you guys..." And another splash of water bounced and dripped off the head and brim of his stained, blue hat.

"You're lucky you didn't get the cooler, but we'd rather drink that."

"Ha, ha, ha..!"

"Just think if that was Vet's Field that's not a homerun."

"Think he would have caught it at Vets?" The coaches asked each other.

"I don't know."

"Who cares...? It happened in Willoughby Hills and that's all that matters."

And after coaches Manta, Billups, and Charles took a few moments to meet with the available parents, suggested:

"Okay boys. We're gonna' go around the corner to McDonalds...sound good?"

"Sweet...can we get one of those warm apple pies there?"

"Yeah, think so..."

"Apple pie...? Get a Big Mac or a Quarter Pounder and fries."

"I'll get a Big Mac and a pie...and some coffee!"

"Do you drink that shi...stuff?"

"No, not really, but it might be good with the pie..."

"Don't get carried away, boys, just get a burger and fries and a small drink...money's tight don't forget!"

"Yeah, yeah, gotcha' coach...!"

There were a few final chants of "Danny! Danny!" as the players, coaches and parents climbed into their cars to laugh and celebrate at the local McDonalds...to add to the modest "billion" or so served, in 1979.

"Yeah, yeah, I finally got a hit…good for me," Grossman said, making everybody laugh at his modesty.

"Dude, that was unbelievable!"

"A coke or sprite is going to go down good!"

"Phew. I sure worked-up a thirst."

"They have seven-up, don't they?"

"Whichever."

"Hey, men, don't forget," Coach Charles said with a smile, sipping on a coke. "We've got one more game…"

"I had my two game day, jumbo waffles again this morning," Stephen Marsch said.

"So did I."

The parents continued taking turns driving their kids when on the rare occasion someone could not make the game's starting time. As the game's progressed it seemed every parent would arrive at some point during the game. The crowds would slowly get larger game after game, win after win.

"Aunt Jemima syrup..?"

"Aunt Jemima syrup," was the reply.

"How does that theme song go…?"

"Oh, no, not again…!" The parents in the front seat were rarely immune. They rolled their eyes.

"Oh, you must mean the Aunt Jemima jingle…?"

"Yes, that's the one."

"Every trip…?" The rebuttal heard from the front seat.

"I'm a Aunt Jemima jumbo waffle eater…"

"Sounds about right…"

"...Breakfast time is so much fun we're always up to greet her..."

"...Talk to me..."

"...In the morning pipin' hot those jumbo waffles hit the spot..."

"...Keep those waffles coming."

"...I'm a Aunt Jemima jumbo waffle eaaa-ter."

"I may never buy those things again," Papa Marsch said from the front seat.

"At least they're not nervous," Mrs. Marsch noticed.

"Oh, dad, we have to pick up some more of that Gator Gum!" Mr. Marsch was a Cleveland police officer previously involved in the infamous "Hough Riots" that had been to Cleveland in the 1960's what the riots in Watts had been to Los Angeles.

"I'm beginning to get sick of baseball superstitions," the elder seed stated looking down the road for a Convenient Store. "If I'm going through all of this to see you guys play you'd better win."

"There's a store! The Gator Gum's a must."

Mrs. Marsch could not help but smile as her husband, exaggerated, shook his head and tried not to do the same, "Freakin' jumbo waffle this and alligator gum that..." He whispered to himself, wanting to be heard.

The Willoughby Hills tournament championship game was played on a Sunday afternoon on Todd Field. Game time was 1 p.m. Their opponent was Willowick A. Euclid's players ignored the fact they had scored 20 runs against Willowick's second team. This would have to be a whole different ball game. And it was.

The game turned into another gut-wrenching pitcher's duel.

Willowick's pitcher – nicknamed the "Falcon" in part because of his last name and his smooth yet aggressive motion on the mound – breezed through six-innings allowing only two Euclid base hits. Both teams traded runs in the top and bottom halves of the same inning. Both teams scored and allowed one unearned run.

The scheduled seven-inning game proceeded to the ninth. Both relief pitchers had allowed one run. The score was dead-locked 2-2!

T.C pitched six-innings; Kenney Richmond pitched three strong through the ninth.

With one out in the bottom-of-the-ninth Casey Urzak walked and promptly stole second base. Harrison Dodd stepped to the plate well aware of his purpose and ripped a line-drive single clear over the shortstops head and into left-center. By the time the outfielders converged on the ball and set to throw the ball in, Casey Urzak had rounded third base easily scoring the winning run.

For the second time a Euclid hitter would be mobbed upon returning to home plate. Harrison Dodd's not as obvious 12-year-old freckles smiled through the stirred-up dust in the Willoughby Hills infield. The players smiled and breathed deeply. The game had felt like a marathon, lasting nine-innings and over 2 ½ hours. They had played a Major League-style game in time and length and had prevailed fighting tooth-and-nail ahead of another tough opponent.

The exhaustive thrill of escaping from the clutches of defeat in the previous game lingered, also. Again, Dan Grossman was slapped on the back and he responded by shaking the hand of another clutch hitter; this one resulting directly in a championship. Harrison Dodd's Tournament-winner would not be forgotten, either.

Within view of Todd Field in Willoughby Hills, officials spoke to and smiled with Euclid's parents, coaches, and a Euclid Sun Journal representative. It was Euclid's second Willoughby Hills Championship victory in the tournaments six-year history.

"You think it might be safe to call them the 'Cardiac Kids'!"

There were laughs. Cleveland's football Browns would arrive at that same "Kardiac Kids" moniker the *following* 1980 September after the NFL season began. Led by quarterback Brian Sipe the Browns would lose the infamous "Red Right 88" playoff game to the Oakland Raiders; the last second interception damning a season that had been highlighted by "Kardiac Kid" style, come-from-behind victories. And by newspaper accounts, the first "Cardiac Kids" reference – and a championship team at that – was the 1979 Euclid Boys League All-Stars!

And Euclid's All-Stars had one more tournament to play. Within the week they would be preparing for their final tournament in Garfield Heights.

THE TWENTY-THIRD ANNUAL IN GARFIELD HEIGHTS

⚜

The Garfield tournament was the longest running tournament in Lake and Cuyahoga County. By comparison, Euclid's Firecracker Invitational had been in existence for just three years by 1979. Garfield's tournament, also, was as large a tournament as Euclid had seen, inviting 32 teams, forcing Euclid to win five games in a row instead of four. Euclid was well aware of the challenge ahead. Garfield had won 7 of the previous 9 tournaments, when hosting. And Euclid, at this point, had become a marked team: everybody would be 'gunning' for them.

The first game was played on August 9th and, again, Euclid's fifteen would cruise to an easy win against a lower-seeded opponent. After the early victory one of the few team photos was taken with Dan Grossman in middle row and center helping to commemorate the game-winning homerun he had hit in the semi-final of the Willoughby Hills tournament the beginning of the month. Plus, in the 2nd round game at Garfield, Dan Grossman – his confidence and stamina fully restored – then pitched three innings to help preserve the arms of "Noose" and T.C. Kenney Richmond also threw three plus innings and Cole Pembroke pitched in his first inning in Euclid's 18-4 route of Independence.

In the opener "Noose" got another win combining on a three-hitter with Richmond, blanking Strongsville, 8-0.

And, it had become more than a rumor that Grossman would not be able to participate for the length of the Garfield tournament. The family had been informed of a sick relative out-of-state and they feared having to leave to attend a funeral. Dan Grossman and his parents would be able to delay travel for some of the tournament, as it turned out, but not for all five games. Before the tournament was completed the Grossman's would be traveling to see family and mourn the loss of Dan's grandmother.

During the same game the news of the illness was shared with the team, Kenney Richmond suffered an ankle sprain bad enough to, visibly, slow him down for a day or two.

Kenney Richmond had slid late into second base off a missed swing on a hit-and-run attempt, rolling his ankle, slightly, upon hitting the tied-in bag, which was something else the All-Stars had acclimated and grown accustomed too since league games, rarely, had bases placed, firmly, in the ground – only at Vet's Field. But, Richmond, hustling and not wanting to be thrown out, slid hard and late when he realized Euclid's hitter was unable to contact the pitch and the throw from the catcher was headed his way. He was safe, but was forced to call timeout while teetering on his back and reaching for his ankle.

Two of the newly assigned, tournament coaches, Schilling and Newton, were on the field immediately to help Kenney off the field, his left and right arm around the two coach's shoulders, demanding he place no pressure on his injured foot.

"Urzak, you're running...Lake you're going to center...! We have to get some ice on Kenney's ankle immediately!"

Garfield had a community park not much different than Willoughby's with multiple fields and a large brick concession stand where ice was readily available. Even the dugouts had the same cover and cement back walls. The players seemed to love the dugouts. They looked the same as the dugouts in *The Bad News Bears* – without the "dugout" steps that descended to the actual benches though.

As great as Veteran's Field in Euclid was it only had a fence enclosure – and no roof! That was the big difference. The walls and not being able to see the fans from the bench gave the players a more secluded, business-at-play mentality. The parents could not walk over and say hello and visit from behind the dugout; there was no waving or smiling or look-at-us gestures during the game. It became inherently more professional, in a sense, within the strategic confines of their tournament dugout while playing for a third consecutive championship!

But, the team was able to rally without the consistent contribution of Kenney Richmond, although he did tie for the team lead in triples by stroking another before the injury. "Noose" continued his, generally, hot hitting by stroking 4 hits including another homerun. He also had a two-run double to help himself against Strongsville as did his soon-to-be starting catcher George Dakalos. Dakalos had been prepped and well prepared for Grossman's departure, catching some when Grossman pitched, for example, and other random innings late in games. Together the Euclid catcher's were, consistently, preventing the opponent from advancing on passed balls or stolen bases; and having Bob Shuman as a third-string catcher had turned into a strong-suit on Euclid's roster. Shuman was a proven catcher and could handle any pitcher as far as speed, velocity, make-up, and movement goes. The only reason he did not start was because his batting average was lower. Behind the "dish", though, he was equally as competitive and fundamentally sound.

Every starter had at least one hit against Independence with Sam Brocco and Tommy Lotts – his swing back – collecting two hits apiece. T.C had two more hits against Strongsville. The middle of the lineup continued its success even without the presence of their five-hitter, Kenney Richmond for one game.

Euclid cruised to an easy win over Lakewood, setting up a rematch against a team hungry for revenge and a return to the championship status that had been taken from them in the Firecracker Invitational: South Euclid was the next opponent.

At the time no one dwelled on the already growing historical significance of these games. Not to say the teams involved – Euclid specifically – were oblivious, but the mounting victories and multiple championships were downplayed. No manager, coach, parent or otherwise ever suggested how rare an achievement this could become – at least not collectively to the players. The coaches knew but, again, chose not to dwell or implore the team to do what no one had done before. Plus, the coaches did not feel it was necessary to add any pressure to the post-adolescent, pubescent ball players. The coaches had no desire or wish to jinx or curse the favorable good vibes and protective mojo that appeared to exist at the core of the team. There was no need to add a psychological "goal" to the already brewing chemistry.

If it wasn't broke there was no need to add anything to the mixture to fix it.

"You know I think I heard…?"

"Don't say it," the players could not help but hear a hint or two of what they were accomplishing. "I heard something too but I don't want to talk about it."

"Kind of like the pitcher in baseball when he's throwing a no-hitter…nobody talks to him about the no-hitter."

"Exactly…! We've said enough already."

"I hear that."

The players simply knew they loved winning and it was their job to continue doing the same. Win! It was certainly much more fun than the alternative. All the other added superlatives and history making possibilities were bonus gravy, after the proven fact and victories were complete.

The Euclid Boys League "Giants" manager, Mr. Menkovich, had taken the reigns as acting Manager for the Garfield Invitational. He did not consider asking the Grossman's to change their minds about the funeral. He would thank his Giants player, Dan, for playing in the tournament and offered his condolences before they departed.

"See you soon...God bless."

Joining Coach Menkovich were Coach Schilling, the Red Legs manager, and Coach Newton from the Yankees. Coach Newton used to make the players laugh because he would tell them not to call him "mister" Newton. "I'm not that old." He would tell them. He was twenty-three. "My dad is Mr. Newton." His father had been a Euclid Boys League manager and officer for years and was directly responsible for the actual purchase and construction of the Veteran's Field concession stand. Even Coach Billups – the other youngest coach of the tournament games – was eight years older than Coach Newton.

"Hey coach!" Casey Urzak had said when seeing his Yankees manager, again – but for the first time as an All-Star coach. "Good to see you."

"Hey, buddy, good to see you too!"

Mr. Schilling drove his Red Legs representative to the next game with his son and bat boy, Denny. The coach's hair was still black and cut short while his son's hair was sunned-light and buzz-cut.

"It's fun being able to coach you kids...especially the way the regular season went."

"I know what you mean. We just didn't have the pitching to compete day after day. And no four-hitter either, really."

"We're playing better now though," Coach Schilling said of the Red Legs. "It's giving me a good feeling...I probably won't lose my temper and leave the game like I did earlier in the year."

"You got our attention...don't forget we came back and won that game..."

"I do that sometimes." Coach Schilling was still referring to his early exit that did not include being ejected by an umpire. He had just become tired of seeing bad baseball and too many losses.

"We weren't playing well, to say the least." 'Kuiper' laughed. "But, the All-Star team is ..."

"You kids are doing alright."

"Yeah, dad, don't do anything stupid," Denny smiled at his dad's visible nervousness. He was 8-years-old. They were getting close to the field.

"Hey, boy, don't give me any of your lip...I outta'...!"

And coach Schilling concentrated on the road and the semi-final against their instant rival, South Euclid.

REMATCHES
AND THE FINAL GAME

❦

August 16, 1979

South was vocal during infield practice, fired-up and ready for a chance to play the team that beat them in Euclid's Firecracker Invitational championship game. It had been a full, impatient month in waiting.

The visiting team scored in the top of the first on a base-hit by South Euclid's rangy four-hitter scoring their lead-off hitter from second. It was the first time a team had scored on "Noose" in the first-inning, but there would be no more scoring until the bottom-of-the-second.

That was when the wheels quickly came off the revenge omnibus.

Two-errors, two walks, and multiple hits later, Euclid's nine had battered and batted around, circling the bases for a nine spot! The game for all intents and purposes was over by the top-of-the-fourth when South's four-hitter could not deliver a hit with two runners on base and the score remained 9-1.

"Noose" Nusman cruised through six-innings and Coach-Manager Menkovich was able to save his ace for an inning if needed in the final.

The opponent would be Maple Heights another team set on exacting revenge for losing in the 4th of July tournament – 7-4 – too Euclid. And Maple had defeated the host team, Garfield, securing their finals appearance by scoring early and hanging-on for the semi-final victory. It was said Garfield had attempted to save their ace, "Owens", for the final in the hopes of a second chance at Euclid. But it had backfired. The early deficit against Maple had been too large for Garfield Heights to overcome.

But, either way, the final game would have to be more competitive than Euclid's semi-final.

"That doesn't mean the game *has* to be close," Coach Schilling reminded.

But this one would be close from the first pitch to the last.

When Kenney Richmond arrived the following day at Garfield's championship field, parents in tow, showing no signs of a limp, Coach Schilling and Coach-Manager Menkovich approached their star player.

"How do you feel?" Coach Menkovich asked Kenney.

"Good."

"Are you ready to pitch today?"

When the young man did not hesitate and seemed honored by the offer Mr. Menkovich added, "Good, you're starting."

Euclid would proceed to draw first blood after Maple Heights stranded two base runners in the top of the first. In the bottom of the inning a base hit from T.C scored Tommy Lotts who had walked. It was 1-0 after the first-inning.

There would be some dramatic firsts in the game for Euclid, good and bad.

Euclid's second baseman let a ground ball get through him for his first error in tournament play. He was so shocked the players had to remind him to forget about it, "It's early."

"Relax Kuip'...get the next one."

He continued to talk to himself in the dugout. The error had resulted in a run and allowed Maple to take a 2-1 lead heading into the bottom-of-the-third.

Euclid came back.

After Harrison Dodd had walked, Sam Brocco singled to score Dodd from second after an out. The score was tied at two. Maple's starter, pitching carefully to Euclid's three and four-hitters, walked T.C and "Noose" to load the bases. Kenney Richmond, showing no major signs of a turned ankle, followed with a sacrifice fly and Euclid led again, 3-2.

It did not last long.

Kenney Richmond did not appear to be laboring but he was not displaying pin-point control. He walked his third and fourth batters of the game and Maple responded with a sacrifice bunt and a two run base hit to re-take the lead at 4-3.

In the bottom-of-the-fifth Noose would strike with his bat, again. He connected on a towering homerun easily clearing the 200 ft. sign and Euclid had tied the game at four.

Players from both sides actually wondered if he had hit the ball 300 feet!

But, it only counted for one and Maple responded, again.

Kenney Richmond's only chink in the armor was the home plate umpire's strike zone. It was consistent, but tight. Richmond's sixth walk resulted in another run and Maple would collect two hits to score two runs in the inning and the lead was 6-4 heading to the bottom half of the sixth.

And George Dakalos then responded by swinging at the first pitch he saw lining it over the left-field fence for the catcher's first tournament homerun! There had been talk the hitters should be sure they were swinging at strikes, since the umpire was calling a small zone. The laser shot surprised and exorcised what doubt remained in the two-run deficit. They trailed by just one run, encouraging Euclid's team confidence once again.

Stephen Marsch, following careful instruction, drew a five-pitch walk and the tying run was on base.

Euclid's second-baseman stepped to the plate wanting to atone for his 3rd inning error. When he was ahead in the count most felt he would take a strike but the pitcher grooved a fastball and the diminutive, bespectacled infielder lined his first extra-base hit of the tournament into the gap in right-center that Maple's centerfielder cut-off on one bounce before reaching the fence. Stephen Marsch's aggressive, head's-up base running – running on the ping of the aluminum bat – scored from first as "Kuiper" anchored his foot to second base, watching Maple's catcher retrieve the relay throw a step in front of home plate.

Euclid had tied the score at six, much to the delight of its fans crowded around the fences and the stands by the third base dugout.

"Noose, you're going in."

Euclid's players could feel the momentum and the confidence completely shifting in their direction.

It was the top-of-the-seventh. The score: 6-6!

And Noosed warmed to the spotlight and pressure by disposing of Maple Heights in order. Euclid exploded off the field ecstatic about the possibility; what was beginning to feel like the inevitable.

Euclid's players – upon exiting the field – could see the crowd growing in number, including coaches Mason, Manta, Billups and Charles from the Euclid and Willoughby tournaments.

Coach Sherwin seemed to smile knowingly through his thick, Fu Manchu mustache.

"One's all we need!" Coach Newton clapped.

"Tim, get ready, you're gonna' bat this inning...Cole you too."

But, they were not going to hit for Jay Nusman in the 7th. The lefty wasted little time stroking a lead-off single to center.

"Remember make him throw strikes!" Coach Menkovich reminded.

Euclid knew Maple could not use their ace since he had thrown seven innings the previous game. One run was extremely plausible, especially with the tight strike zone.

Maple's second pitcher exhaled to remain calm. The count went 2-1on Pembroke and he bounced into a force play for one out.

"That's okay!" Coach Schilling said. "Good contact."

George Dakalos came through again with a base hit after waiting for a strike. Stephen Marsch followed. He worked the count full and ball four was in the dirt putting Marsch on base, again. Maple's pitcher caught the throw from his catcher, snapping his glove downward in disgust, visibly upset.

The Maple Heights manager called time and walked to the mound to talk to his struggling pitcher. He was their last option. It was up to him to finish the game.

Tim Lake swung his bat in the on-deck circle, smiling. It was his first at-bat of the game. And he smiled, twirling the bat above his head.

"It's over boys!" He continued confidently looking into the dugout to be sure his teammates heard him.

"Be smart up there...!"

"Don't be too aggressive...!"

"All we need is...!"

And Tim Lake smiled, and knocked the doughnut off his bat, and nodded to everyone as he stepped towards the batter's box. The meeting on the mound was over. Tim chewed on some – Gator Gum?

"Play ball!"

Lake crouched in his stance and teased the strike zone with half swings and circular motions with the barrel of his bat. The pitch came: Ball one!

Timmy Lake heard the calls and the common sense pleas of a struggling pitcher and a shrinking strike zone – especially for any pitcher on the mound in a championship game, bases loaded situation. Tim Lake held the bat with one hand on his back shoulder, for a second, and crouched in his stance, again. He acted like he was ready to step into the pitch and crush it when it arrived – but he did not swing as the ball sailed passed his shoulders. Ball two!

Euclid's third-base dugout rose in volume! Parents clapped and some did not want to razz the Maple pitcher. That was not good sportsmanship. The Maple Heights pitcher inhaled and exhaled.

"C'mon he's not swinging!" A plea or two came from Maple's defending infielders.

"Let them hit it." Maple's coach instructed.

The next pitch was a strike! The count was 2-1!

Tim Lake looked for a sign from his third base coach.

"He doesn't want to swing!"

Coach Menkovich looked-in at his player and touched his index finger to his nose and to his ear and to the brim of his cap; and repeated the motions: nose, ear, and brim of the cap. And he clapped twice. All Euclid's players saw the sign. They hoped it would not put Timmy Lake in too big a pressure-filled hole – if the pitch was a strike.

The pitch arrived across the shoulders. Ball three!

Euclid's players were all on their feet. Clapping and cat-calls of wildness could be heard from the third base dugout.

"Keep your fingers out of the fence," Coach Menkovich reminded his players of the safety issue. "Be smart Tim."

Coach Menkovich proceeded with his finger to his shoulders, left and right, and to his chin, back to his shoulders and to the brim of his cap. He clapped twice again. The signs did not mean anything this time. It was up to Euclid's hitter. He readied in his perpendicular stance and waved his bat with some restraint toward his opponent. Maple's pitcher wound and threw the 3 ball and 1 strike pitch. The catcher tried to pick the ball before it hit the dirt.

Ball four! Cole Pembroke practically skipped down the third base line, jumping, as Timmy Lake flipped his bat towards the Euclid dugout to look at his teammates, hands in air and jumping towards first base.

Euclid slapped high fives in their dugout. Euclid's coaches yelled to be sure all Euclid's base runners touched their respective bases – and home plate – and the noise level continued when the umpire took off his face mask to officially announce the game was over. "Good game." He said to whoever might here him.

"Noose" Nusman got the win in relief – his third win in five games in the 23rd Annual Garfield Heights Invitational. Kenney Richmond received kudos for "gutting out" six innings on an ankle less than 100%. The team – and team they had been– reveled as long as they could at their accomplishment. "Noose" slapped hands, again, with T.C, Euclid's #2 pitcher for the most part of three tournaments; and the three-hitter in every game; plus the third baseman or shortstop when not pitching. It was decided not to honor anyone with an M.V.P award. It was a close call, in a way, between the players. A vote did not seem necessary. And Mr. Menkovich asked the players to remember Dan Grossman and what he had done and say a prayer for him and his family which everyone did without hesitation. And good luck to Michael Blake and his contribution and their new life, elsewhere. The players raised their heads.

"Ahhhh Menkovich...!" And Coach Schilling and Coach Newton laughed at the spontaneity and the confused surprise on the Manager's face almost asking without a saying word "was that my name they said...?"

The players got to walk through an individual trophy brandishing ceremony. Naturally, non-stop smiles all-around.

Maple Heights was applauded, also, for their second place trophy.

They managed to nod in appreciation. They acknowledged the joy in Euclid's players, coaches, and families. After all, Maple Heights had been a worthy opponent. They, certainly, because of their effort, were instrumental in the festivities taking place on that Garfield Heights Championship field.

The close games made the championship more fun than the blowouts. Nothing done easily is quite as appreciated as something accomplished by hard work; by individuals working together, as a team, with the requisite intestinal fortitude needed to succeed – and/or win.

The opponents shook hands after the final trophy was handed out. To the amateur baseball player this act of ritual sportsmanship had been taught and become an act of traditional instinct. No hard feelings. One team was better for a day. Life and the games would go on.

And, then, Euclid's All-Star coaches began to suggest – definitively – to their players just what had been accomplished that summer of 1979.

"You might want to save some of those Euclid Sun Journal articles," Coach Menkovich suggested. "We should be in the next, weekly addition..."

EPILOGUE, AFTERWARDS, AND A FOOTNOTE

On August 8th, 1979 the National League's Cubs would upset the favored American League Athletics in the third game of a best-of-three Euclid Boys League World Series.

This playoff ended just about the same time Euclid's All-Stars were beginning play in the final tournament in Garfield Heights. Coach "Billups" and his one All-Star would defeat Coach "Mason" and his four All-Stars. "Kenney Richmond" was unavailable for the World Series rubber match on the 8th but he returned by the 9th to play at the start of the Garfield tournament (where he would promptly turn his ankle hampering his play for a Garfield tournament game). "Stephen Marsch" would pitch the third game for the A's after Richmond had lost 2-1 in game #2 to the Cubs and pitcher "Cole Pembroke". The Cubs pitcher in their game #3 clincher was the manager's 11-year-old son, "Walter Billups".

The Cubs had been forced to play a tie-breaking, National League playoff against the Braves whose All-Star rep was "George Dakalos". They, too, lost to the Cubs in a best-of-three.

By the time the Cubs were winning multiple playoff games to win the Euclid Boys League World Series they ended the season with a 17-7 overall record. The A's would not have to participate in a single playoff game before the World Series after 16 regular season games – they won the first and second half in the American League – and the two losses in the best-of-three doubled their loss output for the season. But, the Cubs won the "ring" and rightfully so (The Cubs would be singled-out and honored on Euclid Boys League day at Cleveland Municipal Stadium while attending a Cleveland Indians game). Such is part of the fun and unpredictability of baseball. As with team sports there is more to finding a way to win than just pure, over all talent and athletic ability. It is one of baseball's many under-appreciated nuances.

Like in football on "any given Sunday" baseball has that same sense of aura; and an originality of its own. Baseball, after all, is the only sport or game when you have possession of the ball when you are on *defense*. That is why the pitcher is the most important element of the game. And, arguably, his catcher – the additional "coach" on the field.

No other team sport is played more by "feel" than baseball. It is in its way, really, timeless. Even volleyball has set times for pre-game warm-ups and between periods so the match may proceed at its three or five set pace. Timeouts are timed. Baseball has no time restrictions (as long as the game can be played under lights, of course, and not called due to darkness). All team sports – football, basketball, "soccer" – are based on clock management. Baseball, simply, is not.

Baseball, in its own right, is a timeless, beautiful, easy-going game to watch. Chances for an offensive player are limited to about four plate appearances per game and in the field a position player could go an entire game without a ball hit or thrown in his/her direction. But, when the time comes and the ball is finally headed toward a fielder that player must be prepared to stop and start on a "dime" and get to the ball and not make a mistake. Mistakes must be held to a minimum in all sports but especially in baseball. In a sport where a player can fail 7 out of 10 times and be considered successful a defense does not want to allow that percentage to improve by allowing extra outs. Mathematically, then, a pitcher throws more pitches and, normally, will become tired sooner. Like a base-on-balls the error is just as devastating – if not more so.

Baseball, while not similar in style like football and soccer, is as visual a game to watch on its green grass and turf "diamond" surfaces – in much the same way as golf and its finely manicured fairways and greens and water hazards, and sprouting bush and trees visit the sight lines – the baseball field takes a creative shape of its own along with the dirt and grass that has become a part of its natural appeal, as well as the new construction and feel of "the old ballpark" standards (at the Major League level) and their traditional early, twentieth century advantages; hot dogs and stadium mustard (Cleveland's!); peanuts and Cracker Jack included.

And it can be difficult to describe the feeling the first time a fan sees the inside of a baseball stadium and the awe of witnessing that baseball diamond and the dimensions of the homerun wall surrounding the green outfield; everything a compliment of each other; as well as the advent of the groundskeepers geometrical advancement of precisely dragged infield dirt and manicured grass; and the perfectly straight, thick, white fair/foul chalk lines.

It rates up there with the feel a player has playing on an, actual, grass infield for the first time, after playing strictly on dirt for years. An athlete and tennis star may equate it to the feel that person receives playing on Wimbledon's grass court for the first time. There is something – almost inexplicably – wondrous about its meaning; and its natural and manicured beauty. It – just – is special; and – especially Wimbledon's case – historic.

It is somewhat surprising some people see baseball as boring when there really is so much to see; and so much than can happen.

Baseball is America's past time for good reason. The 100 hundred plus years of history has a lot to do with that, of course, but a fan would like to think an American past time does not place the majority of people watching, fast, into slumber. A true fan is aware of the sports long American history. Baseball was already gaining popularity as early as the Civil War. Soldiers would play a very close relative of today's baseball on both sides of the Mason and Dixon line. By 1887 the National League had developed into a paying "professional" game, although gamblers and fixing games was, already, becoming a controlling, backwards developing influence. And, by 1887, pitching overhand was made mandatory by rule with the hitter no longer requesting – by rule – where he wanted the "underhand" pitch thrown, high or low. The game had grown from its last form of gentlemanly appeal. Not just a game, any-more, it was becoming a business forming into a way of life; an American pastime. There are, certainly, far worse things. And, again, winning can cure plenty; and prevent some evils. To get a non-believer involved in just one hometown team's "Pennant Race" – especially at the professional level – could dispel the misnomer that baseball is boring.

Expectations breed excitement.

And, somehow, this just might help to explain way many agree baseball is the best sport to be listened too on the radio. It offers the use of imagination.

Baseball – occasionally referred to as the thinking man's game.

⚜

Maybe one of the most amazing achievements of the 1979 Euclid Boys League All-Star team is what so many of them never did achieve, athletically. Not one of its players played beyond AA Minor League baseball and only one came any-where near that level of play.

One player was successful at the college Division III level – more notably in football, than baseball, at Case Western Reserve.

For the most part all their athletic careers ended at the high school level with nine of these players attending Euclid

High School where, during the 1984 and 1985 seasons, they were teammates at the varsity level. This was something the players had aspired too, since Euclid High School had already become synonymous with baseball and a traditional power in NE Ohio as a perennial state championship contender.

Tom Murphy became the most prominent and successful Euclid baseball player – as far as pitching at the Major League level is concerned. He would have his most successful seasons with the, then, California Angels who drafted him in 1968 – nine years before Euclid's All-Stars were ten-year-olds. He would start 112 games over a three year period with a career high 243 innings pitched in 1971 (to show how much the game has changed that is an average of 37 starts a year without throwing a play-off inning. Today's "star" pitchers start 32 games in the regular season – at best; hard pressed to receive five more starts – unless their team can continue to win in the post season). He would play for five other teams after 1972 basically becoming a relief pitcher – he would start 15 games the rest of his career – and saved 40 of his 59 games over a two year span with an impressive 1.90 E.R.A in 1974 while playing for the American League's Milwaukee Brewers (they had not switched leagues yet). Tom Murphy also attended Ohio University to ensure his legendary Euclid and Ohio status. He was a senior on Euclid's 1963 State Championship baseball team.

From 1959 until 1993 Euclid High School would need to employ just two head baseball coaches: Bob Addis and Paul Serra. They totaled over 800 wins including the Division I

State Championships in '63 and 1982. They made the finals in consecutive years in '78 and '79 and Euclid would appear in their last final four in 1990. It is safe to say Euclid's successful run in baseball was about as well respected and documented as Massillon and Cincinnati-Moeller would have dominating 30-plus-year runs as Ohio High School football powers.

Chris Spielman – the college hall of fame Ohio State linebacker and NFL stand out – is, arguably, the most popular and successful football player to attend and play at Massillon High School and its proud, football stadium named after legendary Ohio State University and Cleveland Browns football coach, Paul Brown. Spielman went on to star at Ohio State (where he had 20 tackles in Earle Bruce's final game as coach, beating Michigan) and played linebacker for the NFL's Detroit Lions and Buffalo Bills qualifying to play in four pro bowls while in Detroit. His team record 206 tackles in 1996 with the Buffalo Bills was not enough to get him one last invitation to Honolulu.

That would be his final full season in the NFL.

Spielman would be deterred by a spinal injury and his wife, Chris's, much publicized bout with breast cancer. She lost her fight at age 42, but their courage helped bring a new awareness to the topic as well as a growing respect for the athlete who would stand tall by his wife's side. Football became secondary and Chris Spielman could not help but be admired and honored by all concerned.

During a two year span – ending in 1985 – six of Euclid's 12-year-old All-Stars would, also, be "Panthers" on the Euclid

High School football team. They would become part of a local, historic football victory over cross-city rival Saint Joseph's who would claim Desmond Howard – a Super Bowl MVP with the Green Bay Packers – and Elvis Grbac who – as well as Howard – played for Michigan (gasp!), which heightens the dislike of any NE Ohio rivalry. Saint Joseph's High School basketball team would graduate Clark Kellogg who, at least, attended and excelled at Ohio State before becoming a number one draft pick of the NBA Indiana Pacers. Although none of the above mentioned Saint Joseph Viking players were part of the class of '85 team the Euclid football Panthers defeated that year, it was their first football victory over their arch rivals since the early 1970's!

There would be brief reminders amongst themselves of their undefeated run just six years earlier, as "little league" baseball players. But, by then, it had already begun to feel like a lifetime ago. And, for the most part, they had all moved on living in the present to what lye ahead, as their futures would become more viable, pertinent and more clear. It should be noted when asked about the All-Star team and the three tournaments – player, parent and coach – always remember one moment first: "Dan Grossman's" homerun in the seventh at Willoughby hills. It was without a doubt the defining moment.

As for some of the other players, even in this day and age of internet and Facebook, it is not known whatever became of "Michael Blake" after moving or "Sam Brocco" who also moved, apparently, before ever attending Euclid High School – or the cuticle chewing "Christy" from the 10-year-old squad.

"Tim Lake", somewhat ironically, moved and became a Mayfield "Wildcat" where he played basketball and/or baseball becoming a Greater Cleveland Conference rival to Euclid's Panthers.

"George Dakalos" would get to know "Stephen Marsch's" sister and they would marry a few years after high school.

Coach "Newton" remained involved in baseball and runs and schedules tournaments in Lake County to this day (2011).

Coaches "Menkovich" and "Billups" continued coaching at the next level, Euclid's Pony League, and again had success in local round robin and double-elimination tournaments.

And the original Los Angeles Dodger Garvey, Steve, would seriously taint his Mr. Clean, family man image by fathering a child or two (plug-in joke here, if you hadn't already) – infidelity his extreme course of extended action – proving not much is sacred these days.

And it is still not known if the Garfield pitcher was related to Jesse Owens – or his coach-father, for that matter?

It was resolved that the Garfield centerfielder who gallantly attempted to preserve his team's victory – injuring himself in the process – did not maim himself permanently. His back and appendages all survived the "fence" ordeal in complete walking and running capacity.

❦

As a footnote the mention of Garfield winning 7 of the previous 9 Garfield Heights Invitational Tournaments in 1979 was an anachronistic interpretation. They had won 7 of 9 tournaments before – and it is certainly possible they could have achieved such homespun success again – but the reference was actually from a 1966 Euclid News Journal when no other newspapers clippings could be found during the attempt to "factualize" the story as much as possible. But the 7 of 9 tournament wins actually occurred from 1957-65. Again, some creative license liberties were taken to simplify the spirit of the story at the moment being described.

Upon further Euclid Journal research it was discovered "Michael Blake" threw his no-hitter in the first game of the Willoughby tournament proving he did not move *that* early. To risk not changing too much of the, mostly, factual story it was decided to give him his due in the Euclid tournament along with the fact he really could hit too! He was also given an "extra" double in the Euclid tournament which had been struck early in the Willoughby tournament but, either way, he was given his due. Plus, it was never definitively discovered if the regular season team "Blake" played on was the Orioles. By a process of elimination that may be correct. And for dramatic purposes (so it could be written in the *...Athletic Controversy* chapter) the Championship game, final scores in the Firecracker Invitational and the Willoughby Hills Tournament were switched so the Athletics manager (Coach "Mason") could carry *his* Athletic All-Star – "Stephen Marsch" – off the field in Euclid instead of Willoughby Hills because Euclid was the tournament that Coach "Mason" participated. Coach "Mason" – the A's manager – was the one who believed in "Stephen Marsch" from the beginning and *should* have been the one to carry him off the field, symbolically and physically. Plus, he is one of the coaches remembered posthumously.

Most importantly, in regards to this story, these games and these wins did occur in the summer of 1979 (and '77). Hail to the victors...! Oh, wait, that's that "team up north ...!" There will be no more mangy-wolf-on-a-vine (or Pennsylvania's steel town for that matter) mention here. Not from this Ohioan. The only good thing to come from Fishigan is Vernors ginger ale – that and the Bell's Brewery. They're good. O-H-I-O! That's more like it: To the simple pleasures like the clean drinking water in northeast Ohio (really, it's true) and the Great Lakes Brewing Co.! We always look forward to their Christmas Ale!

Cheers and salute, diehard sports fans! Five tournament championships and 21 game win streaks are impressive – at any level!

✣ Euclid's Boys League All-Stars ✣

AUTHOR BIO

Euclid's Boys League All-Stars is the Author's second novel, the first to be Based on a true story. Bruce Double'u has one other novel (of pure fiction) titled Urban Townes.

www.ingramcontent.com/pod-product-compliance
Lightning Source LLC
Chambersburg PA
CBHW072027040426
42447CB00009B/1770